DOG TRAINING, FLY FISHING, & SHARING CHRIST
IN THE 21ST CENTURY

*Empowering Your Church to Build
Community Through Shared Interests*

TED HAGGARD

OLIVER
NELSON

THOMAS NELSON PU
Nashville

A Division of Thomas Nelson, Inc.
www.ThomasNelson.com

D1166322

Words of Praise for

DOG TRAINING, FLY FISHING, AND SHARING CHRIST IN THE 21ST CENTURY...

Ted Haggard points us to creative partnership with the Holy Spirit. It is Him—God, the Spirit—who is seeking to mobilize the body of Christ for penetrating ministry into every corner of the marketplace and community. Here's a tool to help us respond to the present thrust of the Church's ongoing *reformation* touching the world through the everyday people in Jesus' Body.

Jack W. Hayford,
Chancellor-Pastor
The King's College and Seminary
The Church on the Way

This book is a must-read for all who aspire to lead in the Body of Christ. Ted Haggard's practical, refreshing, and vastly enjoyable ideas are important and relevant to the senior pastor, the small-group leader, and everyone in between.

John C. Maxwell, Founder
The INJOY Group

I truly believe that the local, Spirit-filled church is the most important and influential gathering in any community. It is also the key to revival, evangelism, and discipleship in every community throughout the world. In Ted Haggard's marvelous new book, *Dog Training, Fly Fishing, and Sharing Christ in the 21st Century,* he explains the simple, yet powerful strategy any church can adopt to achieve this wonderful purpose God has set before it. I am excited to see how He will use it to impact many ministries and lives!

Dr. Bill Bright
Founder and Chairman
Campus Crusade for Christ

Ted Haggard's new book is a home run! Rarely do we get treated to a book on an old subject (small groups) that opens a window for a whole set of creative dynamics (free-market groups) based not on speculative wishful thinking but rather on measurable success in a real live local church. This book does all of that and more!

C. Peter Wagner, Chancellor
Wagner Leadership Institute

Applying free-market principles to ministry, Pastor Haggard has discovered a formula that has not only worked exceedingly well for his congregation, but that promises to help any church grow, prosper, and minister more effectively today. I highly recommend Dog Training, Fly Fishing, and Sharing Christ in the 21st Century to anyone interested in having a more dynamic church!

Bill McCartney
Founder and President,
Promise Keepers

Ted Haggard, the pastor of the dynamic New Life Church, Colorado Springs, has written a profound, but practical, book that will revolutionize the inner and outer workings of the contemporary Church. As church leaders, the process and production of "Free-Market Small Groups" is destined to transform our forms into functions, our worshiping into witnessing, our learning into leading, and our vision into victories. If you are interested in investing your life into people instead of spending your life on missed opportunities, then *Dog Training, Fly Fishing, and Sharing Christ in the 21st Century* is a must for you.

Dr. James O. Davis
Cutting Edge International
Global Pastors Network
Founder and President

If you are looking for a unique approach to small groups in the local church, this book is for you. Pastor Ted Haggard shares, from experience, a creative vision for a twenty-first century church of greater community, deeper discipleship, and more effective evangelism.

Ed Young
Senior Pastor
Fellowship Church
Grapevine, Texas

In his book, *Dog Training, Fly Fishing, and Sharing Christ in the 21st Century*, Ted Haggard presents a unique cell-group model that empowers church members to bring people to Christ and disciple them in their Christian lives. This model has resulted in exceptional growth in his church. Pastors would do well to consider this model of effective cell-group ministry in their churches.

Dr. Thomas E. Trask
General Superintendent
General Council of the
Assemblies of God

Published in Nashville, Tennessee, by Thomas Nelson, Inc.

Library of Congress Cataloging-in-Publication Data

Haggard, Ted.
    Dog training, fly-fishing, and sharing Christ in the 21st century : empowering your church to build community through shared interests / Ted Haggard.
      p. cm.
    Includes bibliographical references.
    ISBN: 978-0-8499-2897-0
    1. Church group work. 2. Small groups—Religious aspects—Christianity. I. Title.
BV652.2 .H33 2002
253.7—dc21   2002004204

Printed in the United States of America

10 11 QW 06 05

Contents

Introduction

THE CHURCH WORLDWIDE IS HEALTHIER TODAY THAN IT HAS
ever been. There are more Christians than ever before. There are more
local churches than ever before. Parachurch ministry is more effective
than ever before. We have more resources within the body of Christ than
we have ever had. Missionary efforts across the globe are disseminating the
gospel message at an historically unprecedented rate. Christian relief and
development agencies and benevolent organizations are serving suffering
people all over the world. The megachurches of Asia, Africa, and South
America are exploding into supermegachurches, while in North America
megachurches are becoming commonplace. Most cities in the United
States have at least one Bible-believing church that is actively spreading
the gospel. Christian leaders are increasingly innovative and creative at
finding unique, relevant methods to communicate the message of Christ's

love. We have more Christian publications and television and radio stations than our grandparents would have ever dreamed. Christians can be found in every sphere of culture—education, government, business, arts, and entertainment—doing the work of the kingdom.

There's no doubt in my mind: The church is working. We are growing. We are advancing God's message on the earth. Sure, there are improvements to be made, but I believe we are operating from a sure foundation. We have every reason to be encouraged.

Even so, you are holding a book in your hand that is going to try to revolutionize the way you think of Christian ministry. In the following chapters, I want to unsettle many of the basic assumptions we've made about evangelism, church growth, and discipleship in the last fifty years. I want to introduce an approach to ministry that adds a new perspective on the subject. I want to talk about ideas that, while basic and commonsensical to all of us, might be shocking and refreshing when applied to the church.

Why, if things are going so well, do I want to adjust the way we're doing ministry?

There is a popular management book called *If It Ain't Broke, Break It*.[1] This is what I seek to do. Our churches aren't "broke," but I believe they do carry unrealized potential. Things are going well, but they could be going better. When the church I pastor implemented the concepts I'm going to explain here, we were already at forty-eight hundred members. We've since grown beautifully. Years ago our church culture was mostly homogenous. Many of our people weren't as connected with one another as they could have been. Now we have a diverse body of believers who are living in close, dynamic, life-giving relationships with one another. Things were fine before, but now we've discovered a church paradigm that has created a phenomenon unparalleled by anything I've ever experienced. I want to share that paradigm with you.

This book reveals a concept for Christian leadership that will unlock incredible potential in your community. This is a power book. It describes the promise of ministry that is currently latent, but easily accessible, within every church in the world. Just as scientists are discovering new ways to harness power from sunshine, helium, water, and wind, so this book explains how local churches can find explosive ministry in the elements that already exist. I don't want to reinvent the wheel; I just want to show how it can work better than we ever dreamed.

This is not a church-government book. I wrote a church philosophy and government book several years ago titled *The Life-Giving Church* (Regal). To complement that volume, this is a local–church-ministry mobilization book. The ministry style explained in this book will work under any form of church government. In fact, the principles can be applied to any Christian group of people, from a family to a Bible study to a business to a large parachurch organization. In a sense, this is a book about how people work, and about how understanding people will help us unleash the potential ministry that lies within them.

Bill Bright is a major hero of mine. Thirty years ago, a skinny 135-pound teenage Teddy Haggard sat in a stadium in Dallas, Texas, and listened with rapt attention as Bill Bright explained the Gospel. I believed what he said, and gave my life to the Lord that day. Since that time, his life, faith, family, and ministry have been models to me, and I have looked to him as a father in the Lord.

At a recent pastors' event in Orlando, I had the opportunity to spend time visiting with Bill and his wife, Vonette. After that conversation, I believe the four terms that best describe his lifetime of ministry to me are *partnerships*, *lay movements*, *evangelism*, and *discipleship*. As I left Orlando, it struck me somewhere between the complimentary in-flight beverage service and the returning of my seat back and tray table to their full upright and locked positions that these principles explain why many credit Campus Crusade for Christ and Bill Bright for the rapid expansion of the kingdom of God over the last thirty years. These ideas are the core of modern evangelicalism.

That is exactly what this book addresses: unlocking and harnessing within local churches the power of *partnerships* to form *lay movements* in order to establish more effective *evangelism* and *discipleship* in our communities. Whew! Sounds complicated, I know, but it's not. That, my friends, is just the point. It's not complicated, or high maintenance, or exhausting. In fact, it's a philosophy and system of ministry that is wonderfully liberating.

Before we dive in, let me introduce two ideas that you need to keep in mind as you go through this book:

1. *Spiritual authority is important.* The ideas in this book can mobilize ministry in your congregation regardless of the church polity you embrace. We are all submitted to God, and God has delegated His

authority in the earth through four systems of authority: the church, the government, the family, and the workplace. The ideas in this book are intended to complement your ministry within the structures of each of these systems of order.

John Bevere, a close friend of mine and a member of our church, recently published a book titled *Under Cover*[2] that addresses issues of spiritual authority. In the last verse of the Old Testament, the prophet Malachi delivers a very pointed word from the Lord: "He will turn the hearts of the fathers to their children, and the hearts of the children to their fathers; or else I will come and strike the land with a curse" (4:6). Luke's gospel later references this mandate: "'And he will go on before the Lord, in the spirit and power of Elijah, to turn the hearts of the fathers to their children and the disobedient to the wisdom of the righteous'"(1:17). Bevere says that these scriptures address the importance of understanding authority, the "fathers" representing the church leadership and the "children" the body of Christ. A proper understanding of these lines of authority, Bevere maintains, is imperative to a healthy church—and I agree. *Under Cover* addresses the subject of authority to the Body—turning the hearts of the children to the fathers. This book addresses the same subject to the leaders. Its intent is to call and equip all types of shepherds in the body of Christ to love the sheep, to see all the ministry potential that God has put in them, and to empower them to be what God is calling them to be. I hope this book will help turn the hearts of the fathers to the children.

2. *Authority is given in order to serve others.* Many of you reading this book are in positions of authority within local churches, whether you are a pastor, a deacon, or a Bible-study leader. You have a great opportunity to use the authority entrusted to you to serve and to empower the people within your congregation. I am a father of five, which means I'm responsible to serve my five children by praying for them, providing for them, and doing everything I can to ensure that they become the people God created them to be. I am also the pastor of a local church. As a pastor, I am responsible to teach the Word of God and demonstrate the love of God in a practical way. I am responsible to serve others with the authority I have been given, and so are you.

These two ideas are a seat belt for the ride you are about to take. This book strongly advocates creativity and individuality within the church, but I fiercely believe in both submitting to authority and using whatever authority we are given to serve other people. I want the church to be free to run with all the might and potential we've been given under God. To do so, I think we have to revise some of our old ways of thinking. But in order for God to bless what we do, we have to be careful to be respectful, humble, and honorable.

So strap in and enjoy the ride. Find a comfortable place, turn on some music, get a nice drink, and settle in for some great reading. God bless you as you take this journey and learn new ways to share Christ in this twenty-first century.

Chapter One

Purposeful Relationships

I LOVE LOCAL CHURCH MINISTRY. I LOVE TEACHING THE BIBLE, I love seeing the same people every week, I love the friendships I have with my staff, and I love helping people find God's perfect plan for their lives. There is nothing in the world I would rather be doing than pastoring a local church, and I know this is why God has created me. He has blessed me abundantly by giving me a strong, healthy church, a staff of people I love, and a call for my church to make it hard to go to hell from our city.

Even so, it used to be hard for me to think highly of my local church, to really appreciate what God was doing and wanting to do here. Why? Because of my church heroes and the incredible work they are doing. Those of you who are pastors will know exactly what I'm talking about. Do you remember the Saturday morning cartoon called *Superfriends*? You know . . . Superman, Wonder Woman, Aquaman . . . was there anything they couldn't do? Routinely leaping tall buildings, firing laser blasts from their fists with pinpoint accuracy, and deflecting bullets with a lightning-quick reflex of the wrist—they were larger than life. How was any would-be hero to compete in the eyes of a child? Dad, the local fireman, the social studies teacher—all paled in comparison. Likewise, sometimes I've found myself paralyzed by comparison. I've always thought that if only I could be like one of the great pastors, I'd have a great church. I figured the biggest problem with the church I pastor was that I was me and not someone else. You understand what I'm talking about, right?

For instance, I'm a big T. D. Jakes fan. Oh, if I could preach like T. D. Jakes, they'd put me on the cover of *Time* too. But I can't and they don't, so I don't even try.

I also admire Rick Warren. But this guy is much more intelligent than I am, and he gets the benefit of living in southern California. No doubt, if I could think and live like Rick Warren, I'd be set. But I can't and I don't, so I'm not. I feel bad for the pastors who visit Rick's campus or read his book and think they can be a Saddleback Church. Certainly, we have all learned from Saddleback, and I think Saddleback is, without a doubt, one of the bright lights of the future of the Southern Baptist Convention. But Rick is one special man. He's bright, pleasant, articulate, and an ace in the hole when it comes to developing powerful ministry ideas. But, oh brother—if someone told me that to be a pastor I had to be like Rick, I might become depressed. It's just not in my genetics.

Then there's Jack Hayford. Now *he's* my hero. If I could get into a trans-former machine and turn myself into Jack Hayford, life would be wonderful for me. I read his books, study his church, learn his methods, stand like he stands, and hold my hands the way he does, but I just can't get it. His sentences are too perfect for me to understand, much less construct on my own. His knowledge of history is expansive, and his foresight is more accurate than that of modern-day "seers." In my opinion, Jack Hayford is the pastor of pastors in America. He does things right again and again. I would love to pastor a church like Church on the Way, but I can't. I'm not Jack Hayford.

I'm a farm kid. My sentences are often convoluted masses of spaghetti. Sometimes I listen to myself and haven't any idea what I just said, all this while Jack is still qualifying a subtle implication of his basic premise. On some mornings, I would be relieved if I just knew what my premise was, much less be able to qualify the subtle implications of it. So OK, I'm not Jack Hayford.

What about Tommy Barnett? I'm much like him in a couple of ways. Personality? Check. Passion for evangelism? Check. But where does he get his energy? He's up praying before the crack of dawn. His boys look, act, and talk just like him. Everywhere he goes, thousands of people love him. He has a model megachurch and a Dream Center that would take anyone else a dozen lifetimes to build. I go to his pastors' seminars and sit there in awe of this man. He's perfect in my sight. He's happy, spiritual, in love with people, and has time for everybody. It seems as though he can be on television in L.A. hugging his kids while simultaneously orchestrating dragsters, elephants, and angels through his auditorium in Phoenix. I want to emulate Tommy Barnett, but the minute I start thinking about it, I need to lie down and rest. Being in the same room with Tommy gives me vision, energy, and hope. When he leaves the room, though, I take a deep breath and wonder about my inferior genetics.

I could go on and on about my heroes, but I'm afraid now that you're starting to fall asleep. Don't do that. Sit up, take a sip of something legal and becoming to a godly person, and pay attention. Why? Because you've read the books, seen the videos, and attended the seminars of these great men or others whom you respect, and I would guess that from time to time you've wondered why your experience with church isn't the same as theirs. Why do some Christians, some pastors, some church members seem to have it all together, while others don't? Why is church fulfilling for some people, but tiring for others? What is missing from so many of our churches?

For those of you who are my age or older, you'll remember when Dr. Cho's church in Korea shot in attendance from 50,000 members to 750,000 members, and church leaders rushed to Seoul to learn the secret of success. We learned this: Dr. Cho is big on praying, fasting, and cell groups. So across the United States we started praying and fasting, which was great, and we implemented cells, which were a disappointment. They worked to an extent, but they didn't cause our churches to grow the way we had hoped. We did what Dr. Cho did but didn't end up with the world's largest churches.

Church leaders keep trying to be like the greats, which I think is honorable. But too often we find that we don't get the results they do. I feel a little like Philip and Bartholomew. No doubt, it's wonderful just to be in the Twelve, but the other guys seem to get more of the time, toys, and gifts. Where does that leave those of us who are a little more common?

I can tell you. It leaves us sitting in a conference at Willow Creek surrounded by a perfectly tuned ministry machine that is the envy of pastors worldwide. It leaves us watching one more video series on improving our sermons or reorganizing our churches. It leaves us buying one more of their books, attending one more of their conferences, having them pray for us one more time, and then hoping that their systems will work in our lives and in our churches the way they do for them.

Well, I've given up. I just can't do it anymore. In my life, the glossy offers of breakthrough, power, and prosperity translate into hard work, declining strength, and hard-earned promotions. If I have one more person promise me jubilee, I'm going to explode. Do things come easy for you? Or are you like me—do you need to work hard?

This book is for all of you who realize that you are probably not T. D. Jakes, Rick Warren, Tommy Barnett, or Dr. Cho. For those of you who can speak, but millions of people don't rush to buy your tapes, for those of you who can think, but *USA Today* is not quoting you on the front page, and for those of you who can write, but still haven't written a book that's sold more than a million copies, this book is for you. Why? Because I've figured out how average people who are called by God to disciple others in a local church setting can do it with great effectiveness. I'm not special, but the church I pastor is, and yours can be too.

This book is also for those of you who have been dedicated church members for years, and are tired and burned out. It's also for you if you've just begun attending a church and can't quite figure out how to plug in. Or maybe you've been generally pleased with your church, but you're curious about ways to take your membership or leadership to the next level. Maybe you sing in the choir, faithfully attend Sunday school, and contribute to the summer potluck, and are wondering when you'll ever get to rest. Maybe you go to bed every Saturday night hoping you can think of some reason to avoid the awkwardness of church and just stay home and watch football. I've been in every one of those places, and I know how it feels.

In short, no matter what your experience has been, if you want to make church better for you and everyone around you, this book is for you.

CONNECTING IN WADING BOOTS

There is a group of guys in Colorado Springs who get together for fly-fishing every couple of weeks. Early Saturday morning, they meet at one member's home, load gear and food into an SUV, and head into the mountains. Once at the river, they pile out of the car, pull on their waders, sort through flies and rods, and venture into the cool Colorado stream.

To the other fishermen on the river, these guys look like everyone else. They search out a promising hole, cast back and forth, and wait for the snag on their lines that signals a bite. They talk and laugh and enjoy the beauty of the outdoors. But these guys aren't just out for a day of fly-fishing. They aren't just recreating. They're connecting through their local church. In fact, they are holding an officially registered New Life Church Small Group.

At the same time, back in town, people all over the city are meeting for all kinds of different activities. A dog-training group gathers in the city park. Aspiring writers meet in a home to read and to discuss their works, a financial expert coaches a group of married couples on money management, and teenagers meet downtown to serve at the homeless shelter. Men pour into a basketball gym for a pickup game, and women sit drinking coffee and discussing the latest best-selling book at the bagel shop.

What's going on here? These aren't just community groups, although they don't look like church groups, either. But that's what they are. They are ministry groups that have been planned, organized, and covered in prayer. Some of them may never pray or crack open the Bible, but they are an integral part of the ministry of the church I pastor, New Life Church. These groups are as important as Sunday services.

This seems odd, right? After all, what do fly-fishing, dog training, and eating bagels have to do with sharing Christ?

They are ministry, and this ministry perfectly expresses what the Bible is all about: loving God and loving others. When these men are grabbing their rods and boxes of lures to go fishing, the discussions they have will provide as much, or more, practical life coaching than many Sunday-morning Bible classes. The way I see it, *effective ministry is powerfully connecting with God and people—living life better through biblical relationships.* And this is the way Jesus saw it too. Jesus not only ministered in the synagogue, but also while eating a meal, walking down a road, and crossing the lake in a fishing boat with his friends. To Jesus, coaching in the midst of living life together was ministry.

And that's what my ministry is today. I've learned that ministry is not just preaching a sermon, teaching a class, writing an article or a book, and praying with people. Those things are essential but incomplete. The practical integration of biblical principles and godly practice in most people's lives is worked out in relationships. It requires that others grow with them, suffer with them, laugh with them, and enjoy life with them—all while they are intentionally coaching and being coached in life. I believe ministry is connecting deeply with others. Charles Spurgeon, the legendary nineteenth-century British megachurch pastor, wrote: "Communion is strength; solitude is weakness. Alone, the fine old beech yields to the blast and lies prone on the meadow. In the forest, supporting each other, the trees laugh at the hurricane. The sheep of Jesus flock together. The social element is the genius of Christianity."[1]

The genius of Christianity . . . well said. Paul wrote to the church he had planted in Thessalonica, "We loved you so much that we were delighted to share with you not only the gospel of God but our lives as well, because you had become so dear to us" (1 Thess. 2:8). It was Paul's willingness to share life with them that made his message so meaningful. Genuine ministry is about God's will and purpose in the midst of a routine day and average living. It's about understanding the comfort and satisfaction we get from our hobbies and interests as much as it is about preaching and praying. Ministry to some people in our city requires playing basketball, flying kites, snow-boarding, and doing other things people do. It's God in the midst of life.

It seems so simple. To be effective at discipling others in successful living, we have to help others learn godliness in the midst of their very active world.

You see, of all the guys in the fly-fishing small group, only one of them may be a Christian. Only one of them may even know that he is part of a group that is a ministry of a local church. The others may be his co-workers, old friends from college, guys he knows from working out at the Y, or perhaps other men he's met on the river over the years. At some point, he realized that the connection that exists between these men because of their interest in fly-fishing didn't need to be wasted on routine, superficial fish stories. While fishing, these men connected in what could be transformed into positive, intentional relationships that could ultimately lead them to God's plan for their lives.

In time, one, two, or more of the other fishermen will become Christians, and they will invite more men to come, and they will become Christians too. Friends influence friends. A few years of Saturdays on the river in the mountains of Colorado will produce genuine ministry in the lives of dozens of fly fishermen.

And you can bet that most of those guys never planned on setting foot in a church. A humble fly-fishing group has accomplished what an evangelistic outreach would struggle to do: It's connected people in a positive way in order to disciple them in life. Through a common hobby and intentional relationships, lives have been changed.

HOW CAN YOU CONNECT WITH PEOPLE IF THE CHURCH WON'T LET YOU?

The roles of churches are changing. Some are entertainment centers; others are fellowship meetings; and others are teaching centers. Some churches are under so much pressure to compete, to raise money, and to expand that they will do anything necessary to keep people happy. I'm not advocating anything that would cause church members to become self-centered whiners, but at the same time, members often know their personal needs better than we do.

I was raised in the United Presbyterian Church. I appreciate the Presbyterian churches, but I have neither the training nor the personality to pastor a typical Presbyterian church. I was born again under the combined influence of Campus Crusade for Christ and the Southern Baptists. No doubt, the Baptists get a lot of things right, but I don't have the desire to tackle issues the way many Baptists do, nor do I have the patience to work within the Baptist Church structure. I believe Campus Crusade for Christ is one of the best parachurch ministries in the world, but I don't want to perform my ministry tasks through a parachurch organization. I strongly believe it is important for me to receive and to give discipleship within a local church community. And since I believe the gifts of the Spirit operate today, most would think I would like to pastor a stereotypical charismatic or Pentecostal church. But I don't have the energy to lead or attend the endless charismatic services that often accompany charismatic gifts.

Boy, am I in trouble. This is why I highly respect the Presbyterians,

Baptists, and charismatics/Pentecostals, and why I appreciate those who serve in parachurch ministries. They have something that I don't have. What's wrong with me? I don't have the strength or the conviction to minister within these cultures.

What I want is a purposeful and wholesome environment that is simple and to the point. I want a church filled with people who love to grow in God and enjoy one another. I don't want people yelling at me from the pulpit all the time. I don't want to be forced to do a Bible study once a week with people with whom I have nothing in common. Life is too short, so I want to meet and develop long-lasting relationships with people with whom I am able to connect. I enjoy meeting people who like the things I like so we can have exciting, interesting conversations and then turn those interests into relevant ministries.

But I have changing moods and interests. There are times when I want an in-depth Bible study or a rousing discussion about globalization and its impact on completing the Great Commission. But there are other times when I want to talk about scuba diving or just . . . *veg*. (You know—veg out, lie around with friends, eat, and talk about whatever comes to mind. It's what my parents used to call "visiting.") I need a church that will improve my life, not burden it. I need a church that won't wear me out, drain me dry, and then leave me hanging. I need a church that actually helps me. I'm not saying that I need the church to focus on me—I'm certainly not advocating a self-centered approach to church life. But I do want a church that's relevant to life. I work so hard that I need to enjoy church—at least once in a while.

This means that I don't want to leave church beat up and guilty because the pastor expects us to finance every dream he has. The world is already demanding that I buy, give, and serve, so church needs to be a place of refuge from the pressure. I want more than additional work or constant reminders of how I've missed opportunities in life. I want coaching on opportunities. I need to see how to take my situation now and make life better. I need improvement.

I love tithing to my local church, but I don't want to be asked to give more and more every time I go to church. It forces me to say no and makes me feel like a bum when I want to rest in the backyard instead of always being at the church.

I want my finances in order, my kids trained, and my wife to love life. I want good friends who are a delight and who provide protection for my family and me should life become difficult someday. I want a church I can stay in for years. I don't want surprises, scandals, or secrets from my church leaders. I want stability, and at the same time, steady, forward movement. I want the church to help me live life well, not exhaust me with endless "worthwhile" projects.

I don't want to attend a church that sells something to me every time I turn around. If I want to go to the mall, I will go to the mall. The church is not the mall; it's my family. It's where I worship. I'll do my part, but I want benefits too. I want a church that helps me rather than drains me. I don't want a church that wants me because it wants to use me. Don't they understand? I'm tired, selfish, and older than I should be at this age. So I need a church that can give me strength, help me grow, and get me involved in people's lives. I want a healthy church family.

Is this too much to ask?

Apparently not, because I've found it in our church, and other people are finding it in other churches across the world. What they're finding—what we've found—is a way of doing church that makes Sundays a gathering of friends and family, igniting motivation and direction. I can't imagine anything more enjoyable than being with a group of friends to work at expanding God's kingdom while at the same time laughing, telling stories, and experiencing life together. And that's why I love our church. In our church we get to spend time with friends, learn together, grow together, and experience all the dynamics of life together while at the same time being consumed in God's purposes for the earth. We're not living for ourselves. We've given our lives away in Him. But we are living life to its fullest—for Him. *We're using life itself as a ministry to others.*

My wife and I think Sundays are the greatest day of the week because that's when we get to see our best friends. Indeed, I've made a habit of hiring people I enjoy when positions open at New Life because they are the people with whom I want to spend life. For us, every Sunday is a family reunion. I love being with people who know my strengths (and help me develop them) and my weaknesses (and help me manage them). Our offices are full of life because we as a staff actually like one another—so much so that we vacation together, spend time together on our days off, and call one another when traveling around the world to ensure that we share as many experiences together as possible. We often have trouble getting through our staff meeting agendas because we are laughing and enjoying one another so much. We are best friends—we are racquetball partners and traveling companions and aunts and uncles to each other's children. We are doing church—and life—together, and we are loving it.

In short, I think our churches can be the greatest places in the world. We have figured out a few things about how to make church a happy, fulfilling, liberating experience. And whether you're a church pastor, deacon, elder, leader, or a member who wants effective, powerful, and purposeful connections with others in your church, I think the ideas in this book are going to help you make your own church experience better than you ever dreamed it could be.

GOOD MINISTRY STARTS WHERE YOU ARE

What gives me strength is being connected. Do you remember the popular television show *Cheers?* The program's starting song echoes the hearts of so many people: "Sometimes you want to go where everybody knows your name . . . and they're always glad you came . . . " Its appeal was widespread. America was drawn to that mundane little tavern in East Boston, not because of anything unique or flashy about it, but because of how well the people who frequented it knew each other. Remember Sam, the lovable if slightly irreverent bartender; Norm, the endless fount of witty one-liners; Cliff, the kindly postman; and Woody, the naive farm boy, hanging out there together every evening? It was a warm place. It was a safe place. You could expect Sam and Woody to be laughing together. Norm would walk into the room, and everybody would exclaim "Norm!" in unison. Cliff would ask him, "Whatcha up to, Norm?" and Norm would respond with something like, "My ideal weight, if I was nine feet tall." A group of ordinary people living ordinary life . . . together. This is the heart of good ministry—to know people and be known by them. Connecting with people I like and trust encourages me in my faith, sharpens my character, and deepens my understanding of God.

It is this very idea that makes cell groups so appealing. Most of us love the thought of an intimate circle of people who know and accept us for who we are and aren't. What strength, what vitality must be found in such relationships! So what do we do? We arbitrarily group people together and tell them to bond. Study last week's sermon notes. Become friends. Form relationships, because relationships are good ministry. Right? So why hasn't this worked as we hoped?

There's one more thing that we've learned: People connect most naturally with others who are like them. Common interests, ideas, studies, practices, hardships . . . these make the best framework for relational connectivity. Good ministry starts where you are.

Several years ago a man and his wife came into my office. He was dressed "rural conservative" and she was dressed like a Mennonite. They were obviously depressed. They were very kind as they walked into my office and sat meekly and humbly on my couch. He introduced himself as Nate Peachy and his wife as Sheri. Sheri nodded sheepishly and cordially. I hadn't seen people like this in years. They reminded me of the Amish people who lived near Delphi, Indiana, where I grew up.

As is appropriate for their culture, Nate did all the speaking:

"Pastor Haggard, my wife and I have been attending New Life for several months now, contrary to the pleasure of our parents. We're here with our children, and we're all a little discouraged about our ministry. We might have disobeyed God, but we didn't want to. We need your help."

"All right," I responded. "So tell me about how you disobeyed God." (Now, at this point, I was smirking on the inside. I was thinking that these folks just escaped the farm and didn't have a clue about navigating in the city. I was thinking that I would listen to their story respectfully and send them back to country living in Indiana, Ohio, or Pennsylvania. I thought their sin would be something "horrific" like embarrassing their parents by leaving the family community or allowing one of their children to skip Sunday school.)

Nate responded, "We are a Mennonite family. We love the Bible, love our family, and love the church. We felt as though the Lord directed us to be in ministry. Our community agreed, so we tried to plant a church three different times, and each time we failed miserably. Now we're very ashamed. Since we're away from the people who know us, we've started coming to New Life to hide in the crowd and try to discern God's will for our lives."

As I said, I already knew how I was going to counsel them: *Go back home as soon as you can. Life will be easier for you there.* But I didn't want them to be offended, so I decided to make pleasant conversation while I came up with a way to frame my advice. "Do you have any particular interests?"

"No, not really," Nate responded. "We spend all of our time with our family and at church. We don't do much other than those things."

"Have you received any education past high school?" I asked.

Nate responded hesitantly, "Well, yes. I received a bachelor of science degree in chemistry from Grace College."

When he said that, I thought that he was probably a high-school chemistry teacher, so I followed up by asking, "Did you do any additional work beyond your bachelor's degree?"

"Yes," he responded again, looking at the floor. "I received my master's degree and Ph.D. in chemistry from the University of Nebraska."

Now I was shocked. Why didn't he tell me this in the first place? "What do you do for a living?" I asked.

Nate replied, "Well, I just did my postdoctoral fellowship work in chemistry at Los Alamos National Laboratories in New Mexico and now work here in town at one of the high-tech firms."

I couldn't believe it. Now my interest was piqued. I was leaning forward in my chair and wanting to know who this guy was, and why, with a bright mind in chemistry, he would ever want to plant an ordinary church.

"Los Alamos!" I exclaimed. "What were you doing there? Why did the government have a Ph.D. in chemistry working in Los Alamos?"

Now that he saw my interest, a spark came to Nate's eye. He looked directly at me, engaged in the conversation. His wife was excited to see that I was interested in Nate's work.

"Hydrogen separation for fuel cells."

"Fuel cells!" I exclaimed again. "Why?"

"Because fuel cells probably offer one of our best alternatives to the internal combustion engine. They provide a clean source of power that does not rely on fossil fuels."

"Do you work with cryogenics?" I asked. My curiosity was mounting.

"Certainly, we use cryogenics extensively in our experiments—for everything from electrical superconductors to space applications," he said with a twinkle in his eye. "Who knows? Maybe the science fiction ideas of using cryogenics for space travel aren't so far off after all!"

When he said that, the lights went on for me. Sure, it made sense. Since our spacecraft are so slow right now, the only way to explore the solar system and beyond would be to freeze people and let them travel for decades, then thaw them out and let them do their work. I could hardly stay in my chair as I bent across my coffee table, nearly touching Nate and Sheri, and talked to them in whispered but excited tones, knowing that I might be asking for classified information.

"What can you freeze and bring back to life? Can you freeze a chicken? A mouse? An ear? What about a skinny man? A teenager? Tell me, what can you freeze?"

I was so excited about the possibilities of finding out what the government was doing in Los Alamos in its cryogenics laboratories that I didn't give Nate any time to answer between questions. They both started laughing at me. We were all enjoying one another, talking about a subject of interest to all of us, and I could tell he wanted to talk more. But he wouldn't. Instead, with all of us laughing (and with them probably thinking that they needed to send *me* back to *my* family on the farm), Nate got back to the point: "Pastor Ted, we are here to talk about my calling into ministry."

I jumped right in. "Nate, your ministry is within your area of interest. You are a highly respected chemist. You need to minister to people who have a master's or doctorate in science or math, and you need to capitalize on your experience. They will respond to you. For you to open a storefront church and try to have a song service and teach Romans to people who come off the street is unrealistic. It will fail. You need to use who you are, your interests, your experiences, your stage of life, your likes and dislikes to develop your sphere of ministry."

We brainstormed for a long while about what that meant, and over the next several months Nate developed some ideas for himself. Since that time, Nate and his family have blossomed in ministry. Every Wednesday he meets with engineers, technicians, and other highly trained thinkers in the facility where he works in Colorado Springs. Because of his training in chemistry and his background in the church, he is able to minister to people who might never have walked through our church doors.

As the years have gone by, Nate has become a leader of a cluster of small groups and has a ministry that touches hundreds of people each week. He's doing more in ministry than many full-time pastors. His secular training and love for people have combined into an opportunity to serve his community in a beautiful way. He didn't need to plant a church, nor did he need to struggle along in a small traditional church, reaching very few people. Instead, he's fulfilled in his calling utilizing an unorthodox ministry system.

What changed our conversation? It wasn't that I learned that Nate had a more advanced degree; it was that I learned he already had a sphere of influence. He had a natural affinity for the sciences and people in the sciences, but he was trying to "fulfill God's calling" outside of those interests. Helping Nate find God's ministry assignment calling for his life was as simple as showing him that he was already in it.

Living life with Nate and his family is a joy. They are satisfied and stimulated in their ministry. They are ministering to more people than they ever would have as pastors in a Mennonite church, and they are able to spend their days doing what they enjoy and at the same time discipling people with whom they have a natural affinity.

Did you catch that next-to-last phrase? *Discipling people*. As you know, discipleship is one of the fundamentals of local church ministry. We Christians talk about it all the time. So how do we do discipleship? Just as Jesus did, and Paul did, and Peter did, and John did: by knowing people and walking them through life with God's wisdom and understanding . . .

But that's for the next chapter. Now is the time to lay the book on your stomach and catch a nap. I want you to be rested as you go through this book. Chapter 2 is calling you when you wake up, and it will reveal the most liberating discipleship philosophy you've ever read. You will actually enjoy it. It will make you want to stay in church for the rest of your life, I promise.

CHAPTER TWO

Dog Training and Bad Church Services: Rethinking Discipleship

SALLY JOHNSON LOVED DOGS. SHE OWNED SEVERAL DOGS, AND years ago she had become quite skilled in dog training. The Johnson family dogs were all perfectly behaved. Sally taught them to sit, stay, heel, and lie down; she knew how to make them gentle around children and calm while indoors. She knew how to train them to play, to behave around other dogs, and to be protective when they sensed danger. Everyone in her neighborhood knew that Sally's dogs were the best.

One Sunday at church, Sally heard me say that every person is a leader and already has a God-given group of friends that he or she can influence in a positive way. She listened as I explained how God has given everyone the natural ability to be ministers for Him. She couldn't believe it. She was a sharp, articulate soccer mom with a chipper personality. She was living a whole-some, successful Christian life, but she didn't feel she knew enough about the Bible or about church leadership to teach people about Christianity. She knew the Bible and how to apply it, but she wouldn't consider herself a Bible teacher. She never would have felt confident leading a Bible study or teaching a Sunday-school class. Sally was thankful for the church; she trusted me to teach the Bible and appreciated the children's teachers and youth workers because she knew her kids would be mentored and trained as they grew. But she never considered that she could be involved in church ministry.

Soon after, Sally came to our Small-Group Leader Orientation class, where she learned that she could lead any type of small group she wanted. She didn't have to teach the Bible in front of dozens of people or lead intercessory prayer groups in her home. She just had to use her interests to attract like-minded people.

Sally created a dog-training small group in Memorial Park on Tuesday afternoons for anyone who wanted to learn how to train their dogs. She knew some from our church would attend, but because she wanted it to be open to anyone in the city, she placed an ad in the newspaper. On the first day she had seven dogs in her class. (All seven dogs brought their owners to class as well.)

The lessons began. First she taught the owners that their dogs were their possessions, and that they as owners had a responsibility to protect, train, and love them. Toward the end of the first lesson, she began teaching the owners how to walk with their dogs. "Your dog's success is dependent upon your teaching your dog to watch you closely," she explained. "It should walk when you walk, stop when you stop, turn when you turn, and run when you run."

The second lesson built on this principle. Sally taught each student to train his or her dog to recognize its master's voice. Each dog needed to be very familiar with the distinctive qualities of its own master's voice so it would not be confused by the voices of others.

The third lesson was on training the dogs to understand a few basic commands with instant obedience. When a command was delivered, obedience had to be immediate. Week after week, Sally explained all the special dynamics of the dog/owner relationship.

As Sally's class progressed, her relationships with a few of the owners evolved from professional to personal. They would go out after class or on other days for coffee. As these relationships developed, Sally started to explain that just as a dog owner is responsible for his or her pet's care, protection, and training, so God wants to care for us, protect us, and teach us how to walk in His great plan. She began to draw parallels between dog discipline and the discipline of living the Christian life.

For many of these people, the idea of God and how we relate to Him had never made sense. Now, for the first time, the message of Christianity was becoming clear. We need to know how to follow Him; we need to know how to hear His voice. We need to know a few basic commands that are always to be strictly obeyed, and we need to know how to grow in love.

The primary lessons were the fundamentals of successfully responding to God's love in each of their lives. The lessons turned out to be principles not only for the dogs, but also for their owners. This class was a great class on personal discipleship, even for those who hadn't committed themselves to Christ yet.

Sally and her family moved away from Colorado Springs a few years ago, but we still have many people in our church who came to Christ through her small group. From time to time I'll run into people who attend other churches who became Christians through Sally's small group, or who were encouraged in their faith through her ministry. Sally Johnson, a dog trainer in our church who never thought she could do much in the way of ministry, was directly responsible for touching lives and expanding the kingdom of God in Colorado Springs.

This is the model of discipleship I like to teach because it's natural, effective, and modeled from Genesis through Revelation. The principle is simple: People are discipled through relationships, which is why the bulk of Scripture gives accounts of people's lives rather than a more systematic approach to Bible principles. David's friendship with Jonathan, the relationships among Israel's sons, the disciples' jockeying for position next to Jesus in eternity—the Bible reads more like a Dickens novel than a holy book. That God revealed truth to humanity through the stories of people—their triumphs and failures, their joys and sorrows, *their relationships*—testifies to the value He places on being connected to us. The very nature of God Himself—Father, Son, and Holy Spirit, three in one—suggests that He is above all things relational. Most notably, this idea shouts at us through the Incarnation: When God wanted to clear the clutter from our concepts about Himself, He sent a person instead of a text. He established a friendship.

In his fine book, *The Jesus I Never Knew*, Philip Yancey offers insightful commentary on the person of Jesus:

The personality that emerges from the Gospels differs radically from the image of Jesus I grew up with, an image I now recognize in some of the older Hollywood films about Jesus. In those films, Jesus recites his lines evenly and without emotion. He strides through life as the one calm character among a cast of flustered extras. Nothing rattles him. He dispenses wisdom in flat, measured tones. He is, in short, Prozac Jesus.

In contrast, the Gospels present a man who has such charisma that people will sit three days straight, without food, just to hear his riveting words . . . The Gospels reveal a range of Jesus' emotional responses: sudden sympathy for a person with leprosy, exuberance over his disciples' successes, a blast of anger at coldhearted legalists, grief over an unreceptive city . . . He had nearly inexhaustible patience with individuals but no patience at all with institutions and injustice.

Yancey continues on to explore Jesus' relationships:

The Gospels show that Jesus quickly established intimacy with the people he met. Whether talking with a woman at a well, a religious leader in a garden, or a fisherman by a lake, he cut instantly to the heart of the matter . . . People of his day tended to keep rabbis and "holy men" at a respectful distance, but Jesus drew out something else, a hunger so deep that people crowded around him just to touch his clothes.

Jesus did not mechanically follow a list of "Things I Gotta Do Today" . . . He attended wedding feasts that lasted for days. He let himself get distracted by any "nobody" he came across . . . Jesus was "the man for others," in Bonhoeffer's fine phrase. He kept himself free—free for the other person. He would accept almost anybody's invitation to dinner, and as a result no public figure had a more diverse list of friends, ranging from rich people, Roman centurions, and Pharisees to tax collectors, prostitutes, and leprosy victims. People *liked* being with Jesus; where he was, joy was.[1]

If Jesus was anything, He was relational. He was the life of the party, and He was the one who would leave the party to comfort the hurting one. He was the center of attention, and He was the first to give attention to society's most unlovely. He was magnetic, and in the relationships that ensued with the people who were drawn to Him, He was intentional and directional. He seems seldom to have convened Bible study meetings and discipleship groups, but nearly everyone who was around Him changed. Jesus was the consummate discipler.

In like manner, if we are intentional and directional in our relationships with one another, discipleship will happen. Unfortunately it's often difficult to track it, plan it, and describe it in measurable terms. It's not so *quantifiable*, but then, neither was Jesus. It's relational; it's often uncomfortably subjective, but it works.

As I've already mentioned, Jesus communicated God's Word through life. He modeled it and taught it in the midst of living with others. He didn't develop a seven-step strategy for inculcating a list of beliefs into people's minds, which is what we often do with our Westernized, linear approaches to ministry. Please understand, I'm all for linear thinking. As you'll see later in this chapter, I love combining pragmatic approaches and explanations (charts and graphs) with the subtleties of relational ministry. But true teaching, true Bible study, true Christian training happens in the context of real life. It involves getting messy and emotional; becoming involved with people's lives; molding character, values, behavior, and belief systems through everyday experiences. I don't know of anyone who would dispute this. The issue arises, though, in the question of how to structure groups of believers so this can happen apart from the traditional systems that we've all been exposed to in the past.

WHAT DO CLEANING THE DISHES AND GOING TO CHURCH HAVE IN COMMON?

I love it when I'm standing in the pulpit of our church teaching the Bible in a relevant way to the congregation. When I have prepared well and prayed well, the invigoration and satisfaction that comes to my spirit as I do what I'm gifted and called to do gives me an exhilaration that nothing else can provide. I love it!

But I hate it when the opposite happens. From time to time—thankfully not very often—I'll be in the pulpit trying to decipher my notes in front of people who are undoubtedly wondering why I'm off that day. On those days, I get bored with my own sermon while I'm teaching. And if

I'm bored, think of the struggle the people in the congregation must be having!

Part of me wants church to be perfect every Sunday: well-oiled, smooth, and flawless. The songs' pitch perfect; the sermon lucid, theologically correct, historically significant, spiritually alive, and of course, practical for everyone in the auditorium from the ninety-year-old saint to the blue-haired, tongue-pierced junior-high kid. The lights have to be just right, and the carpet should be freshly vacuumed. Oh, life is wonderful in the world of Haggard!

But this is not the way things always are. Sometimes things don't happen the way I want them to—my tongue gets tied, my sermon notes are illegible, the songs don't quite feel right, or the congregation just doesn't seem to connect. Sometimes, whether I like it or not, Sunday services are mediocre. And though I hate those days, I also appreciate them, because it reminds me how church is like family.

We all love Christmas, Thanksgiving, and other special days when the food is perfect, everyone is on their best behavior, and the house is spotlessly clean. But those are not the days that make the family work. Families are strong because of what goes on during normal, average days. I used to call them "bologna sandwich days" until my wife read a book on nutrition and eliminated bologna from our home. Now I call them "clean out the garage days." These are the average days at home—the days when we balance the checkbook, pay bills, and have a normal meal around the table together. These are the days when everyone's had a tough day at work or school and we pour into the living room and crash on the sofas. These are the days when we spend the morning cleaning out the garage and the afternoon playing in the yard or watching a movie. They are the uneventful days. Living these days well makes life right.

"Clean out the garage days" provide a place of peace and safety. They are the times when everything is OK, times when we're all working hard and pulling together to create a wholesome family and a stable, appealing home. These are the days when the fact that we all have the same last name is nice, because it means that even though we are of different ages and different roles, we are all together. And if, by chance, some of us are gone, we miss them and wish they were there. These are the days when Johnny comes home from school, says nothing happened, and goes to play with his friends. These are macaroni-and-cheese days, baseball-in-the-backyard days, fight-with-your-brother-and-then-make-up days, eat-in-the-kitchen days. They don't seem to be anything-special days, you know, nothing to note in the diary. They are the type of days that we soon forget, and at the same time the type of days that we remember for a lifetime. They are the type of days from which life is built.

Families don't fail when they are content with ordinary days, but they do fail when they want every day to be a special day. When parents become full-time entertainers, trying to make every day Christmas, disaster looms around the corner. Good parents understand that the number-one way to ruin a kid's life is to try to make every day a holiday. But if Dad and Mom know how to live well on the average days, their children will grow up to be happy, responsible, solid people, with a rich appreciation for Christmas and an enduring thankfulness for days when the garage is already clean.

Unfortunately, in our ministries and our relationships with others, we often forget to apply this same principle. Even though we recognize that churches are families, we tend to think that to keep them healthy and growing, every day has to be Christmas, Easter, or Thanksgiving. (I know, I know. In some of our churches, the best days are Halloween!) But this can make parishioners like spoiled children, evaluating the services as if they had just been to an Olympic event.

"Today was a 9.9."

"No, I'd give the song service a 9, but the sermon was a 3.5 at best."

If we mistakenly communicate that the purpose of the church's getting together is to hear the most profound sermon, or to experience the most powerful altar time, or to enter into the most spine-tingling worship, then we might as well go ahead and enroll in the burnout program at the local mental-health hospital.

I believe there is value in mediocre Sundays. Mediocre Sundays at church have the same value as mowing the grass, cleaning out the garage, and having Beanie Weenies for lunch. Mediocre Sundays, like ordinary, everyday life, are what keeps the family together. We aren't called to be a body of perfect worshipers; we're just called to help one another develop our lives as worship to the Lord.

When average days are lived well, then the special days are unencumbered in their joy. When a husband and wife are faithful to one another on average days, then Christmas isn't confused with the "other woman."

When average days are lived well, the house is in order, the finances are right, and Thanksgiving can be a time of rejoicing for everyone for the prosperity the family is enjoying. If average days are not lived well, Thanksgiving can be a disappointing day filled with awkward moments of silence. Average days well lived provide the foundation for special days to be their best.

I'm not intending to provide a defense for low-quality ministry, but I am trying to articulate one of the roles of steady, consistent, nonflamboyant local-church ministry that is often overlooked because of its lack of sizzle. Quality and excellence are important so that we can live well day in and day out. But experiencing the sizzle factor in every service might end up costing us, just as it does a family that doesn't know how to enjoy a day at home without entertainment.

Now the application. Why am I tying together the value of training dogs and average days? Because solid discipleship happens when life is regular, average, and routine to provide a foundation for a very special God-empowered future. Discipleship isn't exclusively a system or an airtight theory. We can measure some ingredients associated with discipleship, but not perfectly. We can predict it, but not accurately. We have to live it. As church leaders and churchgoers, our job is to live life well, and to do it unto God with a loving attitude toward others. Paul put it this way: "Make it your ambition to lead a quiet life, to mind your own business and to work with your hands, just as we told you, so that your daily life may win the respect of outsiders" (1 Thess. 4:11–12). It's the macaroni-and-cheese moments of life, and lots of them, lived out together with other macaroni-and-cheese eaters (or dog lovers, or fishermen) that form a patchwork, a mosaic picture that over time looks more and more like Jesus. That's discipleship.

DISCIPLING AT EVERY STAGE: THE ENGEL SCALE

Several years ago, James Engel developed what we now call the Engel Scale of Conversion Stages, or The Spiritual-Decision Process.[2] Engel argued that conversion doesn't happen overnight: People may go through several stages over a long period of time before becoming Christians, and several more stages before becoming strong members of a local church congregation. In other words, everyone has a journey to go through in finding Christ and growing in discipleship. Engel's scale codifies that journey so we can track it and learn how to communicate with people at every stage of the journey.

Engel places people on a line with twelve degrees, from −8 to +3 (including zero), where the −8 indicates a person who has no knowledge of the Gospel and the +3 indicates a person who has several years of conceptual and behavioral growth in Christ. At the 0, one is born again.

Here is a summary of the scale developed by James Engel describing the stages of spiritual decision:

−8 Awareness of a Supreme Being, but no effective knowledge of the gospel

−7 Initial awareness of the gospel

−6 Awareness of the fundamentals of the gospel

−5 Grasp of the implications of the gospel

−4 Positive attitude toward the gospel

−3 Personal problem recognition

−2 Decision to act

−1 Repentance and faith in Christ

 0 The person is born again, and becomes a new creation in Christ

+1 Postdecision evaluation

+2 Incorporation into a local body of Christ

+3 A lifetime of conceptual and behavioral growth in Christ

The first time I saw the Engel Scale, it was evident to me that the majority of the discipleship ministries of our churches were directed toward people who were ready to be born again or to those who had already made decisions for Christ. We were very good at communicating to people from −3 to +3. But Christ's commission to us was to disciple the whole world. He wanted us to teach what He had commanded to *everyone*. Very few of our church programs were geared toward people in our community who had absolutely no knowledge of the gospel.

Furthermore, I realized that I personally didn't have much contact with people on the negative part of the scale. Even when I was associating with an unchurched person, there was often an invisible wall between us. The person knew I was a pastor, which made him feel as though he had to watch his language, act like a really good person around me, and address me as "Father" —not exactly a perfect relationship in which to disciple.

But our church members didn't have those issues. They were involved in the greater community, whether through their jobs or volunteer groups or workout clubs. They were connected to people because of common interests, similar stages in life, a common experience in their histories, or compatible personalities. When I saw the Engel Scale, I realized that if our church was going to be effective at reaching all types of people in the city, it was going to take the combined efforts of every type of person in our church.

Immediately, the tone and purpose of my sermons changed. I stopped merely pastoring, and started teaching them all to be pastors. I told them it was their job to pastor the city. And the church, by and large, went for it right away. Sally Johnson, the dog trainer, is one of hundreds of examples of the members of our church ministering to people at every point along the Engel Scale.

According to Engel, a –8 is a person who is aware of a Supreme Being but doesn't have any working knowledge of the gospel. One of the college students in our church loves movies. A few years ago he decided to use his interest in movies to start his own small group. He began advertising on the local public radio station that a film-discussion group would be starting downtown. Dozens of people came, and the group has been meeting and growing every month since. The people who attend this group do not know they are in a New Life Church Small Group, and very often the leader and his assistants are the only Christians in the meeting. But they choose movies with subtle Christian themes or gently nudge the conversation toward spiritual topics. It's been effective at introducing a Christian worldview to a group of people who would never go to church. It's a powerful preevangelism small group and has been very successful at moving people up the Engel Scale toward a commitment to Christ. One member of the group, a pronounced skeptic who works for the local newspaper, has recently begun questioning one of the Christian members about what it means to have faith. She's been coming to the group since the beginning, and she's finally moving up the scale.

A –7 is a person who has an initial awareness of the gospel but hasn't made any personal application. One of the young men in our church is an outstanding snowboarder. His ministry is to take the kids who admire his ability and go snowboarding with them once a week during the spring semester. These kids know they are in a church small group, and the discussions in the van going to and/or returning from the slopes are about God, Jesus, family, morality, and church. Because of the friendships formed in this group, a large number of young men and women in the snowboard culture in Colorado Springs have come to faith—people we never could have reached through traditional outreach methods.

A –6 is a person with an awareness of the fundamentals of the gospel. One of the older couples in our church who has made a significant amount of money through land investments leads a small group for young married couples in the community who want to formulate a financial life strategy. Obviously, in a bustling community like ours, there are many young couples interested in this type of study. The couples who come hear not only sound financial principles, but they also learn that the number-one contributor to poverty in America is divorce. They listen to a well-respected couple talk about how they've based their financial and life decisions on biblical principles. They hear them explain why issues such as character and honor are important to financial success. These biblical principles move the young couples in the group toward a commitment of their lives and finances to the Lord. They build lasting friendships that mold the lives of the leaders and participants alike.

A –5 is a person who grasps the implications of the gospel. Some of the parents in our church have opened home-school small groups to provide classes for students whose parents are home-schooling them. We have small groups for home-schooled students on Western civilization, algebra, civics, history, and many other classes you would expect to see in any strong school. The difference is that in these classes the students are learning about the impact of the gospel on the world and its potential impact in their lives. I know—some of you are thinking that this is what goes on in any Christian school, and that's true to a degree. But most Christian schools are filled with students whose parents are Christians or who are already committed to some Christian values. This is not a basis for these home-school small groups. Parents from all over our community enroll their students in these small groups to supplement their children's education or to provide a classroom setting for their students to coincide with their home-school studies. It's an incredible atmosphere of learning with a Christian edge.

A –4 is a person who has a positive attitude toward the gospel. We have 130 prayer small groups in our church, and several of them make themselves available to our community to come to the hospitals, hospices, and homes to pray personally with people. Obviously many people don't know the Lord and are not affiliated with a church, but when they find themselves in a difficult situation, they appreciate having a compassionate Christian visit and pray with them. These types of visits and prayer meetings have produced countless fruit in our city. And because we don't limit this ministry opportunity to just pastors, more people are going through the city, praying with the sick and befriending them.

(As I was writing the previous paragraph, I got a phone call from a forty-something single man in our church who owns his own business. He's a strong Christian whose life is based on innovation and creativity, and he's feeling the urge to connect with the church and to be more involved with helping people. Now, wouldn't it be wasteful for me to tell a guy like this that he needs to get together with twelve people from his neighborhood once a week to study something that I've prepared? That would be a bad move. It would be a waste of my time and his. He mentioned that even though the church has eight hundred small groups, there isn't one that meets the criteria he's looking for. I told him that we had a Small Group Leader Orientation class meeting next Sunday after the third service, and that if he came to it, he could start a small group next semester tailored to people that are like him. He said he would be there.

Presto! New Life Church just launched another ministry that will build life into a group of people we're not currently serving, and may consequently build our church. It won't drain me, make me tired, or require anything of me. If it goes well, we'll stay out of his way. If it falters, we'll coach him to make his ministry more effective. And best of all, because of his specialized background, he'll be able to reach a whole new spectrum of people that we haven't yet reached.)

Now, where was I . . . ? Oh yes, the Engel scale.

A –3 is a person who is beginning to realize his or her need for Christ. Now we're starting to ease toward the more traditional small groups. This person might want to attend one of the discovery classes that teaches discovering Christ in our lives or discovering our role in His body. There are many groups that meet the needs of people at this point and higher, such as prayer meetings or a small group studying one of the books of the Bible. A person in this position and the remaining ones can grow in any of the groups as he eases toward a commitment to Christ, His Word, and His body.

Some of the women in our church enjoy having neighborhood coffees. They invite the women in their neighborhood over for a "get to know you" coffee. If this goes well, they offer to host another coffee the following month. If things progress suitably, they suggest that the group start meeting on a regular basis for a Bible study or a book study. Often this appeals to the curiosity of a –3 person. She's never been in a Bible study before, and wants to see what it is like, while spending more time with her newfound friends. She can feel more comfortable asking her questions in a nonthreatening environment like this.

A –2 is nearly ready to make a decision for Christ. Again, many of the groups at New Life apply to someone at this stage. Maybe the –2 should join the basketball group to ensure that he's forming friendships with Christian men and women. Another –2 needs to find a group in which she will learn Bible-reading skills and discover how to apply God's Word to her life. There are groups where these individuals can read books by great heroes of the faith, such as Dietrich Bonhoeffer or C. S. Lewis. If they're interested in Christ and are trying to learn more, they'll have a wide variety of groups to choose from that can answer their specific needs.

At –1, the person wants to repent and to place his or her faith in Christ. This is a great time for the person to be involved with one of the larger groups. This individual is about to come into a decision with Christ and may do so any day. In addition to coming to Sunday morning and/or evening services, people in this stage will likely be faithfully attending a larger group consistent with their stages in life—high school or college meetings, singles groups, young-married dinner parties, or whatever. They are becoming regular members of the church, and the relationships they've been forming in small groups are continuing to help them prepare to receive Christ into their lives.

When someone is born again and becomes a new creature, that individual has reached the 0 stage on Engel's scale. Now this person is in the body of believers and is growing. But he or she still has holiness issues, cultural issues, and the normal issues of life to work out. There will be groups for this new believer at every step along the way. He or she will become more confident in the basic aspects of newfound faith (+1), more strongly incorporated into the church (+2), and will make a firm, lifelong choice to follow Christ each day (+3). At some point along the scale of growth, this convert may decide that there needs to be a group that meets a different kind of need or is based on a different kind of interest. We'll help that individual start that group so the whole process can begin again.

Every small-group leader knows that his job is to bring the people in his group up one point on the Engel scale every semester (our groups are separated into semesters to match with the school system). Yes, that is a subjective analysis. Yes, most groups have people in them at a variety of places on the scale. And yes, it is difficult to measure. But it works very well in discipleship. It gives us direction and keeps us purposeful and focused. The point isn't to be able to track growth or to precisely judge where someone lands on Engel's scale—this is just a useful way of discussing the process. The point is that the church has found a way to meet people wherever they are, whoever they are. As you read through the next chapter, you'll see why this was such a revelation for our church, and you will get a clearer picture of the wonderful difference it has made.

All right, so now you understand the important symbol that dog training is, but what about average Sundays? Well, if people are attending church for entertainment, or to hear profound teaching, or to see the great program, the church might develop in an unhealthy direction. But if people come to church for worship and Bible teaching, having already been connected with others in the congregation relationally, then there is an additional freedom given to the leadership to lead into genuine life-giving ministry rather than having to perform in order to keep the church happy and growing.

What made our Sally (the dog trainer) able to disciple others so effectively? She was living life well and was able to communicate that life in a powerful way. So when she came to church, was I under pressure to give her the best sermon she'd ever heard, with the best worship and the most insightful points? No, I wasn't. Why? Because when Sally came to church, she was in worship and teaching, but she was also with her friends and family to whom she ministered regularly through her interests. She never wrote me and asked me why we didn't have more of the greatest, most powerful speakers. Instead she would write me regularly, thanking me for a powerful place of ministry and a healthy place to grow with her family.

We miss Sally and her family. Not because we need their numbers to meet our corporate goals, but because she's a member of the family and is away right now. When I'm eating a bologna sandwich, I wish she was there. And on those special days—like Christmas Day—we always think of her.

CHAPTER THREE

I Love the Idea of Small Groups, but I Don't Want to Attend One

I'LL NEVER FORGET THE DAY I DISCOVERED THAT I DIDN'T LIKE small groups. No, that's not quite right. I liked small groups for other people, but didn't want to attend one myself.

I had called the executive team of our staff together to discuss the church. We had grown to forty-eight hundred people and were a relatively typical church. Our various departments—children, youth, music, cell ministry—would ebb and flow depending upon the current staff in that department, and we were experiencing steady overall growth in the church. We had incorporated cell groups into the church a couple of years earlier, and though nothing major had happened, we were basically satisfied and convinced of the philosophy that supported the concept of cell ministry. We had eighty cells that were studying my sermon outline every week. The group leaders were well trained, and everyone seemed happy with how things were going in general.

I did have one concern, though: Primary church growth was coming from the platform ministry. If people came to New Life and stayed, it was mainly because they liked what happened on Sundays. Our worship and teaching ministries were well-known, and we had strong ministry at the altars. I was glad Sunday services were strong, but I was worried that the church was too dependent upon the strength of those services alone. I felt that the speaking and worship were pulling the bulk of the weight for all of the other departments of the church. I hated that feeling, but I didn't see any evidence that the other departments were adding families to the church. The main services were adding people, and the other departments were helping to minister to them once they had committed to be part of the church family.

Worse, our growth rate was shrinking toward 4 percent. That's not bad—we were still growing—but I have always maintained that a healthy church would grow between 10 and 20 percent each year. More than 20 percent is too high because it is too difficult to assimilate all the new people into the body of the church. Less than 10 percent produces stagnation. As we were talking about this, Lance Coles, our church administrator, reported that we were experiencing a 20 percent back-door rate. We knew 20 percent loss was too much every year, even though a large portion of that was because people were moving. So we started talking about doing a better job of connecting the people within our church.

I began asking detailed questions about the work in each department. We thought through the potential bottlenecks. Why were people not being integrated? The youth program seemed healthy, as did the children's department. Everyone seemed motivated and enthusiastic. There was no clear explanation for the high back-door rate. After some time, we decided that we needed a church consultant to come in and work through these issues with us to see if he could identify the problem.

Then, just as I was beginning to feel optimistic that we would figure out how to make the church grow better, Russ Walker, our small-groups pastor at the time, asked a question that changed my life. It was during another meeting with our executive team. "Pastor Ted," he asked, "do you attend a small group?"

I laughed. What was he thinking? "No, Russ, I don't have time to attend a small group."

"But you encourage the people of our church to attend small groups," he reminded me. "Don't you think they are busy too?"

"Sure they are," I replied. "I know I should attend one. But I'm balancing my time between pastoring the church, writing, raising five children, and traveling. I can't imagine committing to one night a week with my neighbors. In fact, I don't have a clue who my neighbors are."

Everyone laughed. "OK, OK," I said. "How many of *you* can name *your* neighbors, on both sides of your house and across the street?"

Only our small-groups pastor could do it.

"Don't you think we should know our neighbors?" I asked. Of course they did. But before the conversation turned into a goodwill fest, with all of us making empty promises, I asked, "How many of you really *want* to know the people who live next to you and across the street?"

Awkwardly, everyone in the room admitted that they really had no desire to get to know their neighbors. Who had time for such a thing? Given a free afternoon, there were so many things they'd rather do than try to get to know strangers. They all thought they ought to know their neighbors, that they had a duty to, but they didn't want to.

Russ broke through the tension. "Pastor Ted," he asked, "what would it take for you to go to a small group?"

The team burst out laughing. Now the pressure was on. I was being pinned against the wall with the very idea that I had been promoting to the church. For two years I had been preaching the virtues of small groups. And I believed in them—I really did. I just didn't have time to go to one.

Or did I? As soon as Russ asked the question, I knew the real reason I didn't go to small groups was that I had never liked them. I had tried them and had been to several over the years. But they never held my interest, or I never connected with the people in the group. It was easy to be too busy to go to a small group when going to a small group was the last thing I wanted to do. As I was trying to answer Russ, something a pastor friend had once jokingly said to me shot through my mind: "Small groups are a great idea until you attend one. Too many of them just feel like bad meetings."

I confessed to the group how I felt about small groups. Slowly, everyone around the room nodded. No one liked them. No one wanted to attend one. The only one of us who regularly attended a small group was the pastor who was paid to attend, but he insisted that he really liked going. I just didn't believe it.

Something was plainly wrong. We were doing small groups the way many other churches in America were doing them. I also knew, though, that many of those pastors believed in small groups but were having to coax their people to participate, and often they were just like me—not attending themselves because they didn't want to. I knew that if we as pastors were miserable, lots of other Christians must be too. So, Russ's question hung in the air: *What would it take for you to go to a small group?*

Knowing I was in good company, I spent the next couple of hours talking with my team about the answer to that question. The things we discussed were simple but profound, and the conversation produced ideas that would revolutionize the way small-group ministry was done at our church and at thousands of other churches around the world.

SO . . . WHAT WOULD IT TAKE FOR ME TO GO TO A SMALL GROUP?

I Want to Meet with People I Like

The first thing I told Russ is that I don't want to meet with people that I don't enjoy. As I write this, I'm embarrassed because I know that as a Christian I'm not supposed to prefer one person over another. But my old sin nature rages within, and it's true—I enjoy being around some people more than others. Not that the others are bad, but something inside me has a preference. I don't even fully know why, but it's there. As a result, I have to confess, I enjoy meeting with people I like more than meeting with people I don't like as much. I can't believe I am admitting this!

But God, too, liked some people more than others. You may ask, "How can you say that? God loves all people the same." Ah yes . . . *loves*. But He does seem to like the company of some more than others. Uncomfortable perhaps, but it's undeniable in the Scriptures. To assert this is to say nothing more than that God is a person. He has a personality, has preferences, and is stimulated by some things—and some people—more than others. Why did God "speak to Moses face to face, as a man speaks with his friend" (Ex. 33:11)? Surely Moses sought God in an extraordinary way, but, after all, wasn't Joshua in the tent too? And what about all the other Israelites? God was not speaking face-to-face with any of them.

Remember, too, when God spoke to Samuel concerning Saul's successor?

"How long will you mourn for Saul, since I have rejected him as king over Israel? Fill your horn with oil and be on your way; I am sending you to Jesse of Bethlehem. I have chosen one of his sons to be king" (1 Sam. 16:1). I find secretly amusing the scene that ensues:

> When they arrived, Samuel saw Eliab and thought, "Surely the LORD's anointed stands here before the LORD." But the LORD said to Samuel, "Do not consider his appearance or his height, for I have rejected him. The LORD does not look at the things man looks at. Man looks at the outward appearance, but the LORD looks at the heart." Then Jesse called Abinadab and had him pass in front of Samuel. But Samuel said, "The LORD has not chosen this one either." Jesse then had Shammah pass by, but Samuel said, "Nor has the LORD chosen this one." Jesse had seven of his sons pass before Samuel, but Samuel said to him, "The LORD has not chosen these." So he asked Jesse, "Are these all the sons you have?" "There is still the youngest," Jesse answered, "but he is tending the sheep." Samuel said, "Send for him; we will not sit down until he arrives." So he sent and had him brought in. He was ruddy, with a fine appearance and handsome features. Then the LORD said, "Rise and anoint him; he is the one." So Samuel took the horn of oil and anointed him in the presence of his brothers, and from that day on the Spirit of the LORD came upon David in power. (1 Sam. 16:6–13)

Why David? What was wrong with the first seven sons of Jesse? Imagine the dialogue between the prophet and God going on inside Samuel's head! God didn't dislike the first seven sons; there simply lacked the divine flow with each of those that existed with David. (I'll explain divine flow in a later chapter, so just hold on to that question . . .) There is no way out of it—God does love all mankind, but He just likes some people especially. Like every other healthy, functional person, God has His friends.

The same phenomenon is seen in the life of the Lord Jesus. When Jesus went away to be transfigured, to visit with Moses and Elijah, and to hear the very voice of God, the Bible records, "Jesus took with him Peter, James and John the brother of James, and led them up a high mountain by themselves" (Matt. 17:1). *By themselves.* It wasn't by accident that He left the other nine behind. He was going to a meeting of close friends, so that's whom He brought with Him. Neither, though, did His special fondness for these three (and for Peter and John particularly, as we see elsewhere in the gospel accounts) discount His respect and appreciation for the others. Again in Gethsemane, "He took Peter and the two sons of Zebedee along with him, and he began to be sorrowful and troubled." Going into His darkest hour, His "soul . . . overwhelmed with sorrow to the point of death," Jesus wanted His close friends by His side. "Stay here and keep watch with me," He petitioned them (Matt. 26:37–38). This is not some sterile command or militant order, as is so often the interpretation, but rather the desperate plea of a disconsolate Man for the comfort that can be found only in the company of His friends.

It's important to note, incidentally, that God's capacity for close friendship is infinitely greater than our own. He wants an intimate relationship with you and me, just as He had with Moses and David. In fact, His desire is that every one of us would be His best friend. But that's a subject for another book.

Now, where was I? Oh yes, my impassioned diatribe . . .

I know there are saints in the world who will take their time to sit and listen to anyone saying whatever comes to mind, but I'm not that sanctified. If I don't really like someone, I don't want to sit there and act as if I'm interested in what he or she is saying. It just drives me crazy! Now you may question reading this book because you are discovering one of my conundrums in ministry, but I admit it: I don't want to take a night out of my week, week after week, to sit in someone's living room talking with people whom I don't really like. I have phone calls to make, articles to write, books to read, friends to see, bills to pay, and children to hug (not to mention my wonderful wife, who would love to see me at least one more time before I die). Nope, I'm not going to do it. Not in this lifetime. I know it sounds horrible, but that's how it really is—at least for me.

And besides, I really don't want any more friends. (Oh brother, I hope some editor takes this out. I'm losing my mind. No one should ever admit to this.) I'm barely a good friend to the friends I already have, and I have some great friends. So if I'm going to invest an evening, I want to do it with people with whom I have relationships or some interest in. Give me people I like, and I might go. Give me people I don't enjoy, and I'm sure some emergency will come up to keep me from attending.

Russ stopped me at this point in my soliloquy and said, "If you want to meet with people you like, what does that mean? Who are the people you like?" So we all started making a list of the characteristics of the people we wanted to spend time with. None of us was interested in meeting with our neighbors just because they were our neighbors. I thought that made sense: Just because we live in the same neighborhood doesn't mean we have anything in common. I want to be friendly with my neighbors, of course, but just because they are neighbors doesn't mean that I'm going to invest one-seventh of my evenings with them.

We all decided that the people we liked were the people we were already hanging out with. Those people shared some common characteristics. They were often those who:

1. were in our age groups
2. shared a common life experience
3. had the same life goals
4. were working on the same projects
5. demonstrated an attractive personality type
6. had a common need

Why couldn't we just have a group with these people? We already knew them, and they probably had other friends we didn't know who were interested in the same things or were in similar stages, so we could form a group or multiple groups very easily and naturally. But our current small-group system didn't allow for it. We had to meet with certain preassigned people to discuss a certain book of the Bible or sermon topic, and it wasn't interesting to us. Which leads me to the second idea . . .

I Don't Want to Study Something I'm Not Interested In

I told Russ that if I was going to meet with people to discuss something—there are so many subjects I actually am fascinated by, such as the true goings-on at Los Alamos National Laboratories—I would like it to be something *interesting*. I was raised in a church in which all the teachers taught from the same quarterly, and the topics were rarely relevant to my questions or concerns.

There are times when I'm interested in studying a book of the Bible, but there are other times when I want to study some current event or learn how particular biblical principles apply to my area of interest. Right now I'm interested in talking with others who know about how the

Gospel travels along trade routes, and why much of the Islamic world is enraged because of the free trade that America is promoting, and how the new government in Afghanistan will affect the relationship between Christians and Muslims, and if globalization is the real enemy of fundamentalist Islam. In the context of this conversation, I want to talk about whether or not the Israel crisis could become a world war.

Understand, I wasn't interested in talking about these things before September 11, 2001, and I might not be interested in this subject by the time you read this paragraph. But tonight, it's my interest. Gather a group of well-informed people to talk about free trade, the Great Commission, eschatology, and Islam, and I'm there. No one has to talk me into it, because these ideas will help form the world I'm living in for the rest of my life and will certainly impact missions for the balance of this decade. But don't ask me to have a discussion about this with someone who doesn't know anything about it or isn't a fun interlocutor. Right now, discussions on this subject are very important for American foreign policy and for missiology. Thus, it would be loads of fun with the right people.

But this summer I might want to escape major worldview questions and do something fun with my kids and their friends. When school is in session, I'd like to meet with friends during the lunch hour so I don't have to be away from my family in the evening. One year, I might want to be in a group with my wife that relates to our special interests. At another time, I might want to discuss financial investments with other forty-something men. "My interests fluctuate and shift," I told Russ, "but our small groups are always the same."

I began to get a little angry as I thought about some of the quarterly Bible-study sessions I had to sit through as a high-school student because someone, somewhere, said I needed to know the material. "Why do you small-group guys think we're all interested in the same things?" I asked bombastically. "I can guarantee you that most people in most churches are not interested in the same subjects that interest their pastors! And I guarantee you that the average Christian man or woman is not interested in studying boring curricula written in a Christian publishing house somewhere. People want to study or do whatever is interesting to them at the time."

I talked to the guys about how I hated my economics classes in high school. The material was dull, and I think the teachers found it dull too. But years later, when I was old enough to start traveling, I saw some countries that had lush natural resources and yet starving people, and other countries with no natural resources and prosperity everywhere. Suddenly I wanted to know what economic principles create wealth and poverty. I wanted to know how various forms of government affect people differently. Now, as a grown man and leader of a church, I believe it's vitally important for Christians interested in improving the living conditions of other people to know the basics of free-market economics and freely elected governments. If missionaries and Christian workers don't understand these ideas, they might introduce people to Christ and then neglect opportunities to help their lives improve in practical ways. So my interests have changed, and I'd be frustrated if my church didn't let me have a group in which I could learn more about economics and government. If my small group had to feel like a high-school class, I wasn't going.

I need a small-group system that teaches people about the things they need while they are interested in learning them. If people want to learn the book of Hebrews, I want them to be able to learn it. But if something happens in their lives that causes them to want to learn about the struggles of sexual addictions, alcoholism in Christian families, or adolescent development, they need to be able to switch to those subjects. Most church small-group systems don't consider the interests of the people—the system forces the people to adapt rather than adapting itself to the people.

I Want to Be Able to Get out of the Group Without Making Others Feel Rejected

Next I told Russ that if I were in a small group, I'd need easy exit points. In many churches, small groups are easy to get into but difficult to get out of without hurting people's feelings. I hate that. When I am considering getting into a group of any kind, I consider how it's going to feel if and when I ever decide that I don't want to go any longer.

I have always maintained in the church that it needed to be easy in/easy out. If people want to join the church and become involved, they need to be able to do it simply. But if they need to switch churches, I want to assist them in doing so. I know what it's like to be in church with people who don't want to be there. Some folks come to church out of duty, or because they feel an obligation to God, or because someone tells them that since they have come to this church for so many years, they need to continue coming to demonstrate faithfulness. Too often, though, it's better for the church if they just leave. Church members should be in church because they are happy being there, love serving, and are being well fed—not out of strict, uncomfortable obligation.

I'm not saying every service has to be great, and that emotions and entertainment should determine our church attendance. I honor those who attend out of duty and obligation, but they need to settle their issues and enjoy the church and be a blessing rather than do their duty while making others suffer in the midst of it. If people don't want to be in church, they should leave for the sake of the others. If they believe they have a duty to be there, they should smile and serve and make life wonderful for the others. But to attend out of duty and to scowl the whole time is a disaster.

The same is true in small groups. Sometimes people get in small groups, connect in a special way, commit to the group for a long time, and then for whatever reason decide they need to move on. When that happens, the group often pursues them unnecessarily and makes them feel bad for not showing up anymore, so they remain and start to become sour. There's no exit system for people whose lives or interests change. People need to be able to switch or quit groups without feeling guilty. Thus, I told Russ, I wanted a system that would have exit points in it.

"I think people need to know how long the commitment they are making is when they sign up for something," I explained. "I can do anything for ten weeks. If I know it's a six-month commitment up front, I can decide if that will work in my schedule. If I know it's the length of a semester or will last for two and a half months during the summer, then I can evaluate that. But don't tell me that I need to have lunch with these same guys every Thursday at noon for the rest of my life. Nope, that's not for me. I'm not going to sign up for something like that. No way. *Nein*. Not now and not ever. I need a way out."

I made a lifetime commitment to my wife, to God, and to my children. But I'm sure not going to make a lifetime commitment to anyone or anything else with the exception of a few very special friends. I drive American-made cars, have two golden retrievers, brush with Crest toothpaste, wear all-American underwear, and live in a house with a white-board fence in the front. I'm committed to the values those items represent. But I might change someday. You never know. Someday I might drive a Land Rover, switch from dogs to cats, start brushing with a toothpaste that has a variety of colors in it (a ghastly thought for this Midwestern farmer!), try on underwear that would be no one else's business, and remove the fence from my front yard.

My point is that all of those values, though important, are not as important as a few basic commitments. The level of commitment I make to some small groups might be on the same level as the commitment that I have to American-made cars. I want to support American workers, but someday American workers might not produce the exact vehicle I want, or I might decide that they don't care about me when I see them going on strike for more pay or voting as a bloc for the political party that I don't support. Any of these actions might override my support for them and cause me to buy a Toyota or Land Rover or Saab. As I go through life, my interests change, my preferences change, and my values evolve. I want to be able to stay rooted in one church, but I want to be able to transition in the small groups within that church without hurting people's feelings.

If the Group Is Working, I Don't Want Anyone to Mess with It

The last point I made to Russ that day was the flip side of my last point. If I did connect with these folks, and if we did, in fact, become friends, I didn't want someone, somewhere, coming and telling us that we needed to multiply by dividing the group into two or three smaller ones. If we grew as a team, I wanted to be able to meet with the team. I couldn't see the logic of the church's working to build a strong team of people only to tell us that it was time for us to break up and form additional teams.

Of course, I understood why lots of churches did things this way. *The Master Plan of Evangelism* says that we as individuals need to keep reaching new people, and the cell-group theorists say groups should always multiply so they can spread farther and farther out. It sounds great in theory. But in my mind, it feels contradictory for the church to say, "Connect, love one another, and disciple one another," and then to insist that, once successful, we must split up. One of the greatest difficulties we used to have was when we would have to say, "When your group has X number of people, you must multiply." If small groups are for people to connect in, then splitting up those small groups seems to defeat that purpose.

Oh, I can hear it now. You are thinking, *Ted, you are a committed Christian. You are not supposed to be so self-seeking. You are supposed to have given your life away for the cause of Christ. Why are you being so selfish?*

Well, I'm not convinced it is quite as selfish as it sounds. Jesus gave every one of us an incredible opportunity to connect in His body with others so that we can strengthen and serve one another in a spirit of love. When His divine love connects us with others, that connectivity does something supernatural that makes us want to live for the other person's good. It's a miracle the way God connects our hearts to the hearts of other people so we can make each other's lives better. It's His love. He was the one who said that "they would know we are Christians because of our love for one another."

When small groups work the way they are supposed to, people connect in a divine way with other people, and they begin to pray for one another and care for one another in practical ways. Love connects them. Wholesome, powerful, loving compassion and fellowship develop between these people, and those relationships touch other people. True change happens in people's lives. Once that connectivity happens, why would we split them up? Why would we tell them they can't meet together?

I'll tell you why: It's because the books on church theory demand it for the growth of the church. I do believe it sounds good. I know that it works in some cultures and in some churches. Without a doubt, it works for some. But I don't want to be subjected to a system like that. In a certain sense, it is like Communism: It sounds great to the intellect, but when you try it with actual human beings, it's counterproductive.

When people find genuine fellowship with one another through faith in Christ, why not let them continue meeting and empowering one another? Certainly the exception would be if their connectivity is inordinate or has developed into some sort of an unnatural soul tie. But that's not the subject here. I'm just saying that if I'm going to commit to one of these groups, if it works the way it's supposed to and we all begin to coach one another through life and connect in a life-giving way, I don't want the system to force us to break up.

So, as I explained to Russ that day, if you want guys like me in small groups, you'll have to help me connect with people I like, you'll have to let us talk about things we're interested in at the time, you'll have to give us a way to get out of the group graciously if we want to, and you can't tell us that if we're successful and growing, we have to split up.

Worst-case scenario: Let's say I am selfish and moody and scattered. You need to have a small-group system that works for me. Perhaps *having to be* a mature Christian to function in the system explains why so many of us believe in the system in theory but are not compelled to be in a group our-selves. But if we can design a system that works for me . . .

Oh, and by the way, the discussion among our executive team that day wasn't a rabbit trail. We knew as we talked that we were developing ideas that would shrink our back door and make every department in the church stronger. We didn't know exactly how yet, but we knew this discussion of small groups was going to change the face of our church and give us a way to serve more people than ever before. In the next several weeks, it began to become clear just how that was going to happen.

CHAPTER FOUR

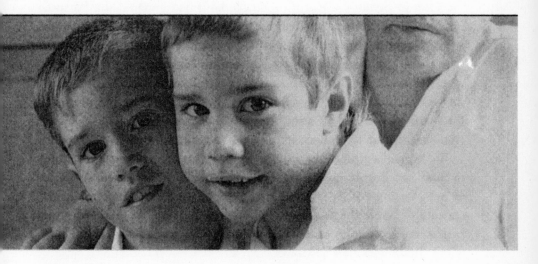

What Do Culture, Economics, and Personality Have to Do with Small Groups?

OUR TEAM SPENT THE NEXT FEW DAYS PRAYING AND BRAIN-storming about a new way to group people in our church. We knew that our current system was stagnant, but we weren't quite sure how to change it. An informal internal market survey of our church made it very clear that people wanted to be able to *choose* a small group based on a clear purpose and sense of relevance—and for a defined time period. We began by look-ing at a couple of models from successful small-group churches: one in Seoul, Korea, and one in Bogotá, Colombia. Many churches in North America had adopted their systems, which were models of tight organization and efficiency, so we wanted to see what we could learn from them to apply to our own small-group ministry.

While we admired those systems, we saw one dynamic in them that we could never replicate: Both churches were filled with people who had experienced extreme suffering, and their small-group systems reflected it. Dr. Cho in Seoul was pastoring people who had endured the Japanese occupation. After they went through the Korean War, these Christians spent their entire lives with the North Korean Communists gazing at them over the demilitarized zone. Dr. Cho kept his organization tight and efficient because he had to, and his people appreciated it. The Bogotá system was similarly well-structured because Colombia had been in civil war for years, and its people were nervous. They needed a strong chain-of-command system to produce stability and security.

We learned a great deal about the innovations in small-group structures in Seoul and Bogotá, but we realized that, like many churches in America, we were dealing with a different kind of people who had different kinds of concerns. Most of the people in our church had never truly suffered. Most had never been hungry except on self-imposed fasts. As far as I knew, most of our church members had never been arrested, never had known a friend murdered, never had their civil liberties violated, never had even driven in a car with bald tires. The vast majority of our congregation lived in nice homes, drove well-maintained cars, worked in pleasant surroundings, and, frankly, did what they wanted to do. While New Lifers were not wealthy by American standards—we are a middle-income church—by global standards they were living in heavenly conditions.

Because our people hadn't endured long-term suffering, we knew they had a different experience of life from the people in Seoul and Bogotá, and they wouldn't respond as well to the kind of top-down, firm leadership that was necessary in those countries. What we were dealing with was what churches in developed countries all over the world were (and are) dealing with: the global expansion of the free-market system and the prosperity and freedom that follow.

Free markets are changing everything. As the markets have created more and more wealth in the world, we've had an entire generation that doesn't know what it's like not to have civil liberties. Our generation has seen a surplus of both food supplies and consumer goods. From Singapore to Paris, an increasing number of people have become accustomed to seeing shops full of products. They are used to having government leaders come and go peacefully, according to the wishes of their citizens. The free-market system has produced a different way of life for millions of people, and with those changes, people's views of life change too.

Are you ready for a brief foray into history? Sip your coffee and perk up, because what I'm about to show you is foundational to understanding why people think, act, and group the way they do today and how we can most effectively minister to them. OK, here we go . . .

The forces that are sweeping the globe and changing the way people do government, business, law, media, entertainment, and just about every other human institution were set in motion more than fifty years ago. At the conclusion of World War II, it became clear that a new international system was taking shape. In his famous address to the nation on March 12, 1947, President Harry S. Truman explained this phenomenon to a weary but hopeful nation:

> At the present moment in world history nearly every nation must choose between alternative ways of life . . . One way of life is based upon the will of the majority, and is distinguished by free institutions, representative government, free elections, guarantees of individual liberty, freedom of speech and religion, and freedom from political oppression. The second way of life is based upon the will of a minority forcibly imposed upon the majority. It relies upon terror and oppression, a controlled press and radio, fixed elections, and the suppression of personal freedoms. I believe that it must be the policy of the United States to support free peoples who are resisting attempted subjugation by armed minorities or by outside pressures.[1]

President Truman's analysis proved exactly accurate, and the policy that he and his successors espoused in response shaped today's world. The second half of the twentieth century saw the world divide into two camps of ideology: capitalist democracy, led by the United States, and Command Socialism, led by the Soviet Union. Conflicting ideologies and the contrasting societies and cultures they spawned (or infested, as it were) defined this period of history, which, of course, we refer to as the Cold War. Well, during the fifty or so years of the Cold War, these two polar ways of life dueled and sparred repeatedly, and ultimately capitalist democracy prevailed.

It's important to realize that America's way did not win out because it *defeated* the Soviet's way. Rather, over time, Communism defeated itself—it came unwound and fell apart—while democracy and capitalism created a better standard of living than the world fifty years earlier would ever have envisioned. Why? Well, there is a library full of doctoral theses written on this subject, but simply put, because *freedom works*. Over time, left to themselves and all things being equal, people would rather choose. Leaders, information sources, dish-washing detergent, whatever—people are wired to respond better, function better, maintain better, grow better, *live better* when they are allowed to choose.

Whew! I'm all fired up now. Give me a minute to regain my composure here . . . Ah yes, now, where were we?

What, you are probably asking, does all this historical commentary have to do with a church's small-group ministry? We realized, as I mentioned earlier, that church members are accustomed to the freedoms to which we Americans scarcely give a second thought. They are used to their way of life, and by and large they like it. They like the benefits, risks, and maybe above all, the excitement of a free-market society. Have you ever switched your toothpaste brand, just for the fun of it? Now think of that secret little thrill you felt on the way home from the store. Come on, loosen up and admit it . . . *What will it taste like? Will it make my teeth whiter? My breath fresher? What if it doesn't work as well as my old standby? Oh well, I can always switch back, or maybe try another brand* . . .

Realizing this mentality, and wanting to work with people's inclinations rather than against them, we set out to harness the forces of free-market capitalism in our ministry. We coined the label "free-market small groups" because we knew that those who enjoyed the lifestyle produced by free markets needed different kinds of small groups than those who lived in either a war environment or under the thumb of some type of central-command economy. I'll explain this in greater detail later, but for now just keep this in mind: We knew we needed a small-group system that addressed the particular concerns of people living under the conditions of a free-market system, and that it would look very different from the systems used in churches in other parts of the world.

Obviously it is important to consider the socioeconomic environment of the members of our church. People in affluent suburban Colorado Springs have a different impression of the world than people in downtown Detroit, so we wanted to come up with a system that would naturally adapt to our church's specific environment. Clearly, I'm opening myself to all sorts of criticism of gross generalization by discussing this here, and I need your grace as I explain these ideas. We weren't trying to label people according to their incomes or whether they had blue-collar or white-collar jobs; rather, we were trying to be sensitive to the various needs of different groups of people. We knew that people who worked at a large factory each day might want different kinds of groups than people who ran their own businesses. We wanted to address appropriately the different cultures we were dealing with. We asked ourselves: Do union workers have different small-group expectations than Air Force officers? Both types of people need the discipleship that small groups offer, but they might respond differently to different kinds of leadership, and we wanted to keep this in mind as we restructured our groups.

THE SMALL-GROUP WILD CARD: THE PERSONALITY OF THE SENIOR PASTOR

There was one other variable that couldn't be ignored: the personality of the senior pastor. It might sound subjective, but we felt that every church should take into consideration the personality of its senior pastor when choosing a small-group system. It's not that the pastor's personality should dominate the church, but the ministry style of the church is impacted by the pastor's personality. If the pastor isn't comfortable with the way people give and receive ministry within the church, then the system is going to have problems, and everyone is going to feel the tension.

All of you have probably taken personality tests at one time or another and likely work with a personality profile system at your job or church. We use the DISC Personality System,[2] so I'll explain personalities according to its terminology, but if you use a different one you'll see the parallels. And, of course, keep in mind that everyone reflects all personality types at one point or another, but each person has a dominant personality that gives him a defining profile.

In the DISC system, *D* stands for *drive*. These people are dominant. They are conquerors. They are take-charge types who love mastering a project. They are generally not known for being touchy-feely. They are task oriented and feel a great deal of satisfaction when they have completed a project successfully. These folks are often demanding and decisive. They can solve problems, are not fearful of taking risks, and don't need someone else to motivate them.

Unfortunately, when they do accomplish a task, there is often a trail of wounded and hurting people left in their wake of accomplishment. Usually they either don't notice that they have wounded people or, if they do notice them, they don't understand why it's a problem. In the mind of the D, people should be happy because the job was successfully accomplished. They tend to believe that the end justifies the means.

Every church has these types of people, and when we place them in the right roles, they get things organized and done. Unfortunately, people with other personality types usually regard D's as unspiritual because their determination appears to be a lack of spiritual sensitivity. D's value time and are often considered rude and out of order. They are not prone to sit around with iced tea and visit about the family all afternoon.

Actually, my heart goes out to D's who are trying to be good Christians, because the church world reads their overstepping of authority and their argumentative attitudes as being worldly. There are some great D's in the Bible: Samson, Noah, the Queen of Sheba, Paul, Daniel, and Joshua. These people knew how to drive a project through to the end.

By the way, this is why I believe Promise Keepers has been so successful. I think Coach Bill McCartney is a D because of his great success and desire to please God. He has learned to temper the negative traits associated with being a D, and capitalizes on its strength. Even so, I doubt that he would be able to, or desire to, climb a normal denominational hierarchy. Even though he is a very considerate man, others are often coaching the coach, trying to get him to be nice. Don't get me wrong—he is one of the most compassionate and considerate men I've ever known, but he's a D—he wants to get things done. He dislikes routine, and from time to time, he attempts to do too much at once. But like many D's, he's gotten great work done for the kingdom of God.

Note: A D's greatest fear is being taken advantage of.

I stands for *influence*. People with I personalities are inspirers, great story-tellers, and strong public speakers, and are usually very likable. They trust others, and are enthusiastic, emotional, and wonderfully (or woefully) impulsive. They motivate people, they smile too much, and they love to get together with other I's just to enjoy one another's company.

These personalities are often the life of the party, and if they haven't learned to temper their personalities, they can be the most obnoxious persons in the room. It's not uncommon for I's to talk too much about themselves and then say, "OK, I've been talking too much about me. So what do you think about me?" (This is the place to laugh.)

They see the glass half-full, never half-empty. They are the encouragers, the ones who cheer others on to success. They connect quickly with people and tend to see positive traits in others. They are creative problem solvers and they use their sense of humor to entertain and encourage. They seldom tear others down. They love to love and to be loved. They are often effective peacemakers. I's embrace change; they are attracted to adventure, and they enjoy people.

But because I's are so excitable and view every request as acceptance and inclusion, they often overcommit to projects and people and are unable to fulfill their promises. Sometimes I's will be so concerned with people's feelings and opinions that they will forfeit tangible results or important details in order to keep peace. Since they are not usually concerned with details, they usually understand the big picture and want others to get it too.

I's talk too much, don't listen enough, and fear rejection. If you criticize a D's work, he or she will try to improve it. Criticize an I and that individual will be devastated. But if you want a champion for a cause, hire an I. The I's in the Bible are Mary Magdalene, Barnabas, and Nicodemus. Aaron was also an I—study him and you'll gain insight into the weaknesses and strengths of a Christian leader with a dominant I type. The Samaritan woman (at the well) was also an I—she brought many people to Christ even though her personal lifestyle was questionable. David, Gideon, and Naomi were all I's—passionate, enthusiastic, and often hard to control.

I would guess that T. D. Jakes is an I. From what I've observed, when he walks into a room, even those who disagree with his theological positions or question his style of ministry enjoy him personally. He's pleasant, a great communicator, and a persuasive champion of the causes he believes in. When he is in the room, everyone knows it. When criticized or when he fails to persuade, though, he's sensitive about it, takes it personally, and tries to convince the critic. With difficulty he can manage others' differing with him, but he's better with it if he knows they are OK with him personally.

It's difficult for him to navigate these conflicting messages because he is such a high I. I think he probably depends upon others to help him articulate the subtleties of theology, history, and other subjects that are detailed because he is strongest with big-picture ideas and can communicate them best. He is very wise and intuitively knows what people think and how they feel. He loves people, and people love him. He doesn't like conflict.

I, too, am an I. That's why I have to be very careful about overcommitting my time or diverting from my schedule on a whim to do something fun or exciting. Personal discipline is hard for me as an I, so my prayer life isn't as systematic as it is dynamic. I, too, am very sensitive to criticism and am too hesitant to tell others, "No." I, too, depend upon others to work out details while I create, conceptualize, and communicate ideas. I love big ideas. I love studying the way people group and how to motivate them to do their best. I enjoy inspiring others to succeed.

Note: An I's greatest fear is being rejected.

An S is a *steady, stable* person (S is for *steadiness*). S's love to listen, and they listen well. S's make up 70 percent of the population, which is what makes our churches, families, and communities stable. S's are great teachers and friends, but they are not flamboyant or risky. They are safe. S's tend to have a few close friendships that are deeply meaningful. S's are understanding and predictable.

I know S's well. My wife, Gayle, is one. So since I'm an I and my wife is an S, I would rather err on the side of saying all nice things about my wife's personality type than to be more detailed and thorough about the S personality, which might create risks for me. Since I'm an I, I say, "Ditch accuracy and create peace, love, and acceptance." (Smile again here.)

S's are reliable, dependable, loyal, and respectful of authority. (How am I doing?) And wonderfully, they are patient, empathetic (which makes them great lifelong friends!), and skilled at resolving conflict between people—most notably in our home between Alex, Elliott, and Jonathan, our three youngest sons.

In any church, the S's have underground networks that question and, if necessary, subtly resist anything that interrupts their security. They are not hard to spot because they are nice, pleasant people who value stability, consistency, and sanity. They are reasonable and logical, often too traditional—not because they love it or believe in it, but because it's safe. They communicate with one another and take on one another's feelings, but are not confrontational, and they love the safety of a steady community of faith. Many S's translate their high regard for security into a resistance to change.

Bible personalities who were dominant S's include John the beloved, Moses, and Eliezer, Abraham's servant. Anna, Jacob, and James (Jesus' brother) were all S's. Note the steady, stable, and subtle influence these personalities have had in history. These people are important in the life of any church.

Reverend Rankin, who was the pastor of First Presbyterian Church of Delphi, Indiana, when I was a boy, was an S. He was a walking glass of warm milk. He methodically visited hospitals and nursing homes. He knew everyone's name, all of their families, and was a consistent influence in the lives of everyone who knew him. His sermons were short, insightful, and packed full of stories and names of real people. He didn't ruffle feathers. He never moved the pulpit or any other furniture in the church; instead he added value and established the purpose for the furniture. He always preached in a robe, always sat in the same chair, and always drove the same car. One time he spoke standing beside the pulpit for a few moments—odd that I would remember that thirty-five years later. He never jumped over the pulpit or stood on a chair to teach. The thought of anything out of the ordinary happening in Reverend Rankin's presence is difficult to imagine. He was a blessing to our family. I remember how he made me feel.

Note: An S's greatest fear is loss of security.

C stands for *compliance*, so a C is one who is *correct* and *correcting*. These are the accountants, brain surgeons, and chemists. C's love details. They love documents and systems. C's are the administrators who develop forms, forms, and more forms. They love red tape. They love precision and accuracy. They are analytical and conscientious. They have high standards because they are precise and systematic.

In our church, we have a C administrator and a C accountant. These personalities keep us realistic and authentic. They are even-tempered and help the team evaluate every situation. They love details and are not argumentative. Their greatest fear is criticism of their work. If you criticize them personally, they'll be fine, but if you criticize their work, you had better have your facts in order.

C's in the Bible are the Shunammite woman from 2 Kings 4, Matthew, Luke, Shadrach, Meshach, and Abednego—people who were consumed with the details of their situations. Joseph, Jonah, Priscilla, and Aquila were C's as well. And of course, Zipporah, Moses' wife, was a C—she got the details right in Exodus 4, which saved Moses' life. We're all grateful for the C in her personality.

Christian leaders who are C's are often teachers or researchers. George Barna is probably a C. He wants to know how to measure whether or not a city is reached, a congregation is discipled, or a person is persuaded. You can't just tell him you are persuaded to be a Christian; George wants to know what that means to you. What do you believe about Jesus? The Bible? The Church? Your personal life? On and on the questions will go. But for George, that probably won't be enough data. So he'll compare your answers to the Scripture and to the answers of others who say they are Christians.

Nope. Still not enough. Now he'll take the combined answers from those who say they are Christians and compare them with those who are not Christians and see if there are differences significant enough to validate sanctification. Gotta love the George Barnas of the world. See the pattern? Men like George Barna and other C's in the body keep the story straight, the reports accurate, the plumb lines in place.

Note: A C's greatest fear is criticism.

From the pulpit, a C will explain the subtle implications of a comma in a certain verse, while the I wants you to feel good about God. The S wants you to feel secure in your faith in Christ, and the D wants to motivate you to complete the Great Commission yesterday. I's often think S's, who love stability, are the resistors to balance the I's, who love change. D's think I's talk too much and don't do enough, while I's think D's need to lighten up and enjoy life. I's think C's make mountains out of molehills and spend too much time talking about the importance of turning in receipts and filling out forms. C's think I's are irresponsible. When an I tells a story, the details are not significant; the main point is. When a C tells a story, accuracy and details are vital, so the story often becomes too long for the I's. S's just want everyone to get along.

People are dynamic, which means that each has a dominant personality type that combines with other personality types to formulate unique personalities in each of us. For example, I am an ID with an ability to be a C. But when I'm home, I'm an S—I just want everyone to get along. So as a pastor, I'm not consumed with controlling others, but rather inspiring them (my I) to be productive (my D) and to live God's best plan for them according to the Scriptures (my C). But when I go home, my S is dominant, so I don't usually want my home to be a party house, but rather a place of peace, safety, and rest.

Interestingly enough, most megachurches are pastored by people with some combination that includes a dominant I or D, while the majority of churches, especially mainline denominational churches, are pastored by people with dominant S or C. Nearly every denominational executive is either an S or a C, usually with a supporting I or D. However, most apostolic network leaders and founders of newly birthed denominations are either I's or D's because their function requires them to be consensus-building activists. I's and D's who can't build consensus are just obnoxious people, in my humble opinion. And S's and C's who can't work with others in a structure are wasting their God-given potential.

Why does the pastor's personality profile make a difference in how a church does small groups? It would never do to force a certain type of group system upon every pastor, because the pastor needs to understand, appreciate, and support the way ministry is mobilized and organized within the congregation. As we discussed this among our team, we theorized that if a pastor was an ID, like I am, he wouldn't be very interested in the details of the small-group meetings, but would be concerned that (1) the meetings were enjoyable and (2) that something was being accomplished. If, on the other hand, a pastor had a high C in his personality, he would want to ensure that the small groups were detailed and addressing something very particular. If the pastor were an S, he would want the meetings to be safe and stable. It's not that the church should do whatever the senior pastor wants, but the pastor needs to be able to understand, support, and propel the system.

DIFFERENT GROUPS FOR DIFFERENT FOLKS

As we discussed all these variables, from culture to socioeconomic group to pastors' personalities, we decided it was foolish to think that any one type of small-group system could work everywhere in the world. Some churches would even have to blend various types of systems to find something appropriate for them.

Oh, I know, it's starting to sound too scattered and complex. But it's not.

The question is: How do you do it all? How do you work with everyone wanting to meet with people they like? How can you have everyone wanting to study the particular subjects they are interested in at the time? How can people possibly leave a group without making the others feel rejected? How can you avoid dividing a group when it gets too big? And how in the world do you take into consideration the various cultures and the personality of the senior pastor?

It sounds like a lot, I know. But it's not hard. We found the answer. And this answer worked so well for us that our back-door rate shrank dramatically. One year after implementing free-market small groups, our back-door rate had fallen from 20 percent to seven-tenths of 1 percent. The vast majority of those who used to leave our church because of lack of connectivity now stay. And our system is both flexible and adaptable enough to allow for frequent change, and solid and predictable enough to ensure that real results are happening. In the next chapter, I'll explain why.

CHAPTER FIVE

Intentional Discipleship

ALL RIGHT, NOW WE KNOW THERE ARE VARIABLES THAT AFFECT the way any specific church ministers to people. We also know that people vary in their own understanding and relationships with God. It's our responsibility to take them, wherever they are, and move them toward a personal commitment to Christ and His Word, and toward a vibrant relationship with a congregation of believers. Any system that we develop needs to be flexible enough to account for all these variables and to attract people with the kinds of idiosyncrasies described in Chapter 3 (that is, people like me!). The system needs to be highly adaptable and changeable depending on the church's needs and wants from year to year.

"But, Pastor Ted," you might say, "this sounds so random. Can you actually disciple people when they are free to discuss any subject they are interested in? Aren't there subjects that people should learn whether they want to or not? The system you use is not really a system at all! It gives people what they want, but it doesn't give them what they need. It's too centered on the individual's wants, and not enough on Christ or the Word. Come on, Pastor Ted, you are describing a party, not a method of discipleship. You need to be more serious!"

Oh, I know. I've heard this all my life. When I was in high school, I attended a little Southern Baptist church in Yorktown, Indiana, that had an average attendance of eighty people. These people were remarkable believers. Even though they had limited resources, they had a great church. There was a good Sunday school that met before the main service and taught from a quarterly Bible study series. Despite my earlier comment about those studies, they were helpful, and we did diligently work through them. This church did a great job of teaching the Bible on Sundays and Wednesdays in the main services, and offered fun activities from time to time, such as pot-blessing dinners, hay rides, and retreats for various groups within the congregation. It was a productive church.

I attended the church regularly, but was also highly involved in my local high school. I had a lot of friends at school who were from a variety of church backgrounds, and some of them didn't have any church background at all. Even though I was a Christian, I regularly had weekend parties at my house with two or three hundred high-school students. Then, on Tuesdays, I would host a Bible study at my house led by one of the local parachurch organizations. Between eighty and a hundred people came to the meeting each Tuesday. It's safe to say that our house was a bustle of activity.

The weekend parties that we had at my house were not godly. They were parties with loud secular music, immorality, drinking, and drugs. And then on Tuesdays, some of the same kids would get together and study the Bible in the same living room of the same house in which they had been drunk the weekend before. At the time, none of us thought much of it. When I look back on it now, I can't believe it. But when I think of where I was as a young man trying to grow in Christ, I know that my life was full of contradictions.

I remember once when the church decided to take the high-school boys to the wooded hills of southern Indiana for a camping trip. There was a beautiful spot just upriver from Metamora, Indiana, that was great for camping and swimming, so we decided to go there. I invited my friends from school, and more than 150 came. We had a great time sitting around campfires telling stories, skinny-dipping, and enjoying all the things that a group of rowdy young men would enjoy at an understaffed, poorly organized church youth camp.

On one night, I gave my testimony of how God touched my life at Explo '72. I explained that since that time I'd committed to read one chapter in my Bible every day, no matter what. Here I was in front of my peers, who knew I was always available for a good laugh, and I was explaining to them that when I went home after having fun with them, I would pull out my Bible and read a chapter every night. I gave the plan of salvation, and we ended up baptizing eighty or ninety of them the next morning after additional training around our morning campfire.

This was rough on my pastor. He didn't like the idea of kids making a commitment to Christ and being baptized until enough time had passed for them to prove that they had actually accepted Jesus into their hearts. He didn't want to baptize them until they had been through a series of lessons at the church so they would fully understand the meaning of water baptism. And he certainly didn't like baptizing them until their parents were fully aware of their decisions and had endorsed them.

I couldn't disagree more. I pointed out that I was a high-school kid just like they were and that our lives were full of contradictions. I told him that I knew that many of these students were sexually active and involved with drinking and drugs from time to time, and their parents didn't know about it. I said, "All of us are doing all kinds of destructive things in our lives that we hope our parents don't know about. We try to keep lots of secrets from them. So why is it that when we finally want to do something good, we suddenly have to wait until we get permission?"

I told him that these were high-school students, not little children, and that they should be allowed to be baptized whether they involved their parents or not. "Come on, Pastor," I urged, "Let them do something right for a change. They get their girlfriends pregnant without permission. Shouldn't they be allowed to be baptized without permission?"

Finally, he surrendered his better judgment and we had a baptismal service. This was around the time of the Jesus Movement, and soon after, many of these students started attending Jesus rallies, youth-group meetings, and Bible studies. So many of them started going to Christian groups that it wasn't long before the spiritual countenance of the school began to change. Bibles were everywhere. Copies of Hal Lindsey's *The Late,*

Great Planet Earth were on every fifth or sixth student's desk. Discussions about sex, drinking, and drugs took a turn for the moral. The primary reason for this shift was not parental involvement or school government activity, but because the students themselves were reading their copies of *The Living Bible* and were working through their own issues in small groups of friends.

Most of these students came from homes that were relatively stable, and many had had religious upbringing. As this trend began in our school, the Catholics kept going to Mass and catechism, and the Methodists, Presbyterians, and Nazarenes kept going to their own churches. But scores of unchurched or loosely connected students started going to church with me at the little Southern Baptist church, which essentially doubled because of the influx of high-school students.

These trends made the school's efforts to encourage good behavior seem ridiculous. I'll never forget when, soon after this, a Planned Parenthood spokesperson came out to tell us about birth control. We essentially told her that when we had needed help, she was not around, and now that we'd decided not to go the route of immorality, we didn't need her services anymore. After her departure, the class told the health teacher that we wanted some representatives of the clergy in the community to come teach us about sexuality. He responded that he thought that would be illegal, so we protested, wrote letters and articles about religious discrimination, and finally prevailed. Soon we had a Catholic priest and a Baptist minister come speak. This was the will of the class—certainly not the will of the teacher, the administration, or the school board—and the Christian leaders had much more practical things to say than the woman from Planned Parenthood.

I'm not advocating against Planned Parenthood or for preachers in public-school classrooms. I am suggesting, though, that the various stages of life people go through will serve as a strong discipling environment. To many, the environment will seem strange, random, unstructured, haphazard, and disorganized. But this is the essence of biblical, relational discipleship. A study program on Christian discipleship would never have worked with my high-school friends and me. This loose, freewill system did.

Of course, there was discipline. The pastor at the Southern Baptist church remained sharp during this time. I remember his getting high-school students together in a circle around him and pelting us with Bible questions: "How many books are in the Bible? What was Jesus' first miracle? Give me an accurate definition of the Trinity. How can we know if we have eternal life? How did God speak to Moses the first time?"

The questions would go on and on. We were made to learn about being born again, being filled with the Spirit, healing, deliverance, and the priestly order of Melchizedek. He taught us the Scriptures and showed us how to live in holiness. But we didn't mind his questions because we had initiated the process ourselves—we were studying the Bible of our own volition and were in relationship with one another and him. He didn't force us into the church program; he made the program fit us.

This happened to me thirty years ago, and though I've lost touch with most of my high-school peers, I am in touch with enough of them to know that their walks with Christ have continued and many of them are in local church or denominational leadership positions today. Why? Because we had a discipleship system that fit our personalities, our culture, and our interests.

Personalities, culture, and interests. Personalities, culture, and interests. Can we have discipleship systems in our churches that fit every member's personality, culture, and interests? Yes, I know we can. We're doing it in our church right now. That is why our back-door rate has dropped. People stay because they find what they need. They find what they need because the free-market environment creates a supply of resources for every possible demand.

And actually, we have no other choice. If we don't disciple people according to their personalities, cultures, and interests, many of our churches will continue on their paths of irrelevance, with plateaued or declining participation from the community.

MAKING DISCIPLES EVERY DAY

In his book *Growing True Disciples*, George Barna challenges old paradigms about discipleship. He lists seven things that are necessary to improve the quality of our disciple-making strategy. His suggestions are to:

1. shift from program-driven ministry to people-driven ministry

2. change the emphasis from building consensus to building character

3. de-emphasize recalling Bible stories; emphasize applying biblical principles

4. move from concerns about quantity (people, programs, square footage, dollars) to concerns about quality (commitment, wisdom, relationships, values, lifestyle)

5. retool developmental ministry efforts from being unrelated and haphazard to being intentional and strategic

6. replace ministry designated to convert knowledge with efforts intended to facilitate holistic ministry

7. alter people's focus from feel-good activities to absolute commitment to personal growth, ministry, and authenticity in their faith[1]

Barna argues that the "things that got us where we are today will not get us where we need to be tomorrow." He explains that to disciple people well, we need "a comprehensive and far-reaching commitment to radical change in how we conduct our lives and ministries."

In other words, we need to leave behind the ultrastructured, overly programmatic discipleship methods of the past. No doubt, many wonderful Christians have been discipled well in these systems. But I can't make them work. When I think about discipleship, I think of long Bible studies with predictable questions. I think of personal character goals and behavioral-spiritual goals. I think of someone giving me a thirty-day plan to increase my Bible study, prayer, and church participation. Just thinking about everything that usually coincides with a discipleship program wears me out.

Of course, the goals themselves have merit. All of these goals are fundamental to growing in a relationship with God and the church body. All of us should be intentional in our spiritual lives, and all believers should work with a team of others to shape their spiritual disciplines. That's why there's always been a strong argument for streamlining the process—we know we need to get them from A to B to C in order to arrive at Z, so we just plan it out step by step.

The problem is that the system is too sterile, so most people won't do it. They say they will; they express interest in it, but very often, they don't participate as promised. Discipleship programs don't often work because people don't stick with them. So we can either push them on people harder, or change the system.

Also, most Christian discipleship programs have two inherent flaws: (1) They apply to Christians alone, and (2) they assume Christian growth is linear. I believe that we are responsible to disciple all the people in our spheres of influence, whether or not they have made commitments to Christ. We have a responsibility to make disciples out of struggling high-school kids in our church youth group just as much as we have a responsibility to disciple people who are secular humanists or just passive about religion. It's our responsibility to disciple those people just as it is to disciple the young Christian, the newly divorced mom or dad, and the sixty-five-year-old who has been in the church all of her life. We have to disciple those who want to be discipled and those who are not fully aware of the fact that God loves them and has a plan for their lives.

But discipling an agnostic and discipling a young Christian are two different things. If we want to disciple a teenage Ted Haggard, there will be some days when he will agree to a mentoring relationship with a mature Christian with set objectives in mind, but there are other days when he's not interested and would rather skip the meeting and go skiing, camping, or biking with some friends. If we want to disciple our workout partners at the YMCA, we can't give them a twelve-week Bible study, but we still need to figure out a way to help them grow in the realization that there is a God who loves them.

And we can guarantee that teenage Ted isn't going to grow in a linear, logical way. He likes Z and wants to get there, but his path won't be a line, it will be more like a river: following the squiggly path of least resistance. Thus, he'll start with A, jump to H, return to B, and then work on Q. Linear, no. Progress, yes. Logical, no. Lively, yes.

So what do we do?

THE FUNDAMENTAL THEOREM OF DISCIPLESHIP

Discipleship = relationship + intentionality

That is the bottom line. Discipling people isn't always giving them programmatic goals; it's purposefully helping them live through every day according to God's plan. It happens in the context of genuine relationships if the people in those relationships are intentional about becoming people of God. Want examples?

Moses' primary disciple was Joshua. How was Joshua discipled? By going with Moses where no one else went. Elijah's primary disciple was Elisha. How was Elisha discipled? By living with Elijah. By spending his days and years with him and by being his servant. Jesus had twelve disciples who learned from Him by listening, watching, and growing together through life. Paul impacted the lives of those around him as they experienced ministry, persecution, prosperity, and suffering.

Often when we read the Bible stories about the lives of these people, we don't realize how intentional they were being about discipleship. But they were intentional. I imagine that as our Bible heroes lived life together, they would identify areas in one another that needed shaping, and they would create opportunities to address those issues in the course of everyday life. Paul modeled the Christian life for everyone around him because he knew they needed to grow, and I'm sure he knew exact areas in which each person needed to grow. In 1 Thessalonians 2:8, Paul says, "We loved you so much that we were delighted to share with you not only the gospel of God but our lives as well, because you had become so dear to us." In 1 Corinthians 4:16, he says, "Therefore I urge you to imitate me." In Hebrews 6:12, the Bible pushes this concept of relational training by saying, "We do not want you to become lazy, but to imitate those who through faith and patience inherit what has been promised." Then the Bible drives this point home with Hebrews 13:7, where it says, "Remember your leaders, who spoke the word of God to you. Consider the outcome of their way of life and imitate their faith."

This is true discipleship. Not only does the Bible teach objective, quantifiable truth, but it also talks about the personal dynamic of living life together, the sharing of life in a day-to-day environment.

I travel all over the world to teach on prayer. People seem to like it, and I trust that it does some good in their hearts. But when I travel, I take some friends, and every morning we pray together. I know without a doubt that after these trips, my friends know how to pray and that they often integrate what they've learned in prayer with me in hotel rooms into the fabric of their prayer lives. Discipleship is a two-pronged fork: training and modeling. One without the other is weak.

So if we have high-school students in our churches who are still working out their personal devotion by reading one chapter of the Bible a day and attending church, more mature believers whose walks with the Lord are marked by discipline and vitality, and others still who are somehow connected to the church but not even Christians yet, how do we disciple them all?

I suggest that our only hope is to teach people to do it the same way Bible characters did it, by knowing people and teaching in the midst of life experiences.

Know People

The Christian message is not exclusively communicated through the dissemination of words. One of the tenets of Christian living is its contingency on personal relationships. The point of Jesus of Nazareth's being the Messiah is that God Himself came to us in the form of a man—someone who could be touched and seen and heard. His message was that we can know God personally. The whole essence of Christianity is rooted in the idea of relationships; thus, personal relationships are fundamental to learning godly living.

Whenever I teach about small groups at other churches or conferences, I emphasize that *everyone is already in a small group.* Everyone already knows people with whom they probably meet on a regular basis—even if it's not scheduled—and nearly everyone meets with a group of people every week. The church's job isn't to rearrange those people; it's to give their groups God's purpose. It's to coach them in the groups in which they already participate or to which they are already drawn. We don't determine which groups people belong in—we just nudge the direction of each group.

How do we do that? It depends on the makeup of the small group. Discipleship will look different for a group of friends at work who enjoy having lunch together than it will for a group of women who meet in a neighborhood for Bible study. A group of guys who are connected because they snowboard together will need a different style of discipleship than a group of older Christian ladies who sew together. The point is that these people already know one another, and they know other people not currently in their groups who would be easy to include. Our job is to encourage those relationships and remind those in the group to be purposeful about helping one another grow in Christ.

Once when I was explaining this idea to the leadership team of a very successful church in Houston, the pastor's wife jokingly spoke out in the crowd and said, "We could have some great mean-women small groups.

We have so many angry women who bicker with one another and try to cover it up that they need a small group to get together and get healed!" Everyone laughed.

To my knowledge, that church didn't do anything with the idea. But soon after in another city, I was telling that story, and one of the ladies who is a counselor picked up on the idea and started offering a mean-women small group for women who had been hurt or wounded and were more angry than they wanted to be. These groups grew and grew, and now this church has a large series of mean-women small groups. Women from throughout the community attend and find a great deal of help in these groups.

Guys, imagine talking with your wife in the morning and having her tell you that she is attending a small group for mean women. You just can't lose on this one. Everyone always smiles, but no one ever reveals whether or not he believes any particular woman should attend. But it provides a great opportunity to say, "Why would you attend a small group for mean women? You are such a great person." Or to say, "I appreciate your willingness to minister to mean women. Of all the women I know, you would be a great model for mean women to discover how to get along with others." Or the mysterious silence that communicates, "Yep, you need a mean-women's small group. Thank God someone finally came up with one."

Anyway, the idea is that these women already had a common bond, and the counselor at that church simply capitalized on that bond, made them into small groups, and made their discussions intentional. But I can guarantee you that mean women aren't going to go to a small group without a friend. People need to be with people they like. They need people who understand them. They need friends. They need an intentional objective, yes, but they need to reach that objective in the midst of a group of friends.

Teach in the Midst of Life Experiences

I was a youth pastor for several years. Today when I see some of those former students and ask what they remember from those years, they never mention a particular sermon or lesson I gave. They all remind me of an incident, an experience, or an occasion when they learned an important life lesson. They remember mission trips and baseball games and evenings out together.

Rob Brendle, one of my associate pastors, told me this story:

I remember one summer mission trip. I went with three teenage boys from our high-school youth group to teach English at a junior-high school in a large city in western China.

The four of us were assigned to a throng of Chinese students, whom we dutifully instructed in the subtleties of American conversational English. Using unmarked pages of Scripture for text, we planted seeds of truth in their minds in the classroom while building friendships with the students after school. The hope was to gain the opportunity to discuss with our hungry new friends the stories we had read together in class. By the second week, Ben (one of my kids) had developed a trusted friendship with Tony, a bright and eager Chinese boy. It was clear that he wanted to know more about what he had read, and that he was interested in knowing the truth. That night in our hotel, I gathered my guys, and we prayed together with overflowing excitement for the conversation we would have the following day.

The next day, Ben and Tony and I found a discreet corner in the public park and sat down to talk. I helped steer the conversation toward spiritual things, gently set the ball rolling, and then sat back and handed it over to Ben. He sputtered and rambled for a bit, reminding me in retrospect of a baby bird newly vacated from its nest and using his wings for real for the first time. There was a twinge of awkwardness in that moment, but thankfully, Tony is Chinese and understood little English at the time, and so the bulk of what was happening was lost on him. Soon, though, Ben started speaking clearly. Empathetically, tenderly, and passionately he shared what the Lord Jesus had done in his life. He listened to Tony's questions and answered clearly, referring him to the story we had read in class the day before about the father who welcomed back his wayward son. Ben shared. Tony absorbed. I beamed.

Tony gave his life to Jesus that day, led in a prayer of commitment by his dear friend Ben. The two kept in touch after that, Tony asking questions and relating struggles of following Jesus in China, Ben encouraging him in his walk. I don't know how Ben would have taken to a prepared curriculum of material that systematically instructs the discipler in leading others to Christ, but I know he will never forget that summer.

More than any sermon on the subject of evangelism, Ben will remember the experience of being coached in life by Rob.

As we read the Bible, we see men and women of God teaching lessons by what they did, not just by what they said. I think that's why the local church must relate as a family. We can't divorce. We need to have good and bad days together. We need to be strong and growing together, and we also need to suffer, make mistakes, and from time to time just be lonely together. A church in Tulsa uses the slogan, "We do life together." I think this says it perfectly. I can teach Bible principles in the midst of actually living life better than I can in the midst of a sanctuary full of people listening to me.

I remember another story of a young couple who came to see one of my associate pastors about a year ago. The wife was the first to come and talk about her concern over their marriage, her husband's anger, lack of communication, etc. She said neither she nor her husband was connected to any other men, women, or couples in a godly way. In fact, she said her husband would probably refuse to do so. When asked if she thought her husband would be willing to come in and meet with a pastor, she had little confidence that he would do so.

To everyone's surprise, they came in together to talk with the pastor. It was obvious that the young husband, though he wanted to be a good husband and father, had really shut down and was almost totally self-reliant, frustrated with his wife, and disillusioned with God. What's more, he wasn't listening to anyone except his own mind.

Our staff encouraged this couple in biblical principles about their marriage relationship, including the need to submit themselves to godly friends. At first, he was not willing to connect with other people—men *or* couples. Nevertheless, he soon committed to attend a couples small group with his wife. Then he decided to attend a men's retreat. There he connected with a few other godly men and started attending a men's small group around a topic that piqued his interest. In the safety of this group, he has made some real friends. As each of his male friends has walked through various trials, he has learned how to model their responses to the same hardships. His small-group leader understands the purpose of the small group for this man: to move him one step closer in his relationship with God.

Now, even through some very trying experiences of his own, this young man is walking close to God and praying with his small-group leader regularly. He is becoming a great husband and a loving father. I seriously doubt if he could list the sixty-six books of the Bible or define the priesthood of the believer, but he is living out his relationship with God day to day alongside other godly men. I'd prefer a life well lived, based on good decisions, to a life full of head knowledge alone.

Small groups need to be available for all age groups, as well as for those who want intergenerational groups. Small groups need to be available for virtually every interest in our congregations. Homeschoolers need something different from those who want to pray for foreign missionaries. If we line people up in rows in our churches and lecture them on godly living and Bible principles, we will teach some—maybe 5 percent. But if we connect our congregation members so that they are doing life together—so they learn how to live when a son disappoints, or when an unexpected death occurs, or when a lush inheritance comes their way, or when a daughter graduates from an outstanding university with honors, or when a tragedy shakes the nation—we'll have a healthy, growing, incredibly close family of believers.

CHAPTER SIX

Why Free Markets Serve People

LET ME GIVE YOU FAIR WARNING RIGHT UP FRONT: IN THIS chapter, I'm going to talk about some ideas that are reshaping the world. You've heard some of them, but I bet you've never thought of how they apply to the church. Stick with me through the explanations in the first half of this chapter. Don't skip to the end. If you understand the foundations behind these principles, it will change the way you think of church and will improve your life and the lives of everyone around you.

Now, let's get started. Since the time of Cain and Abel, mankind has been struggling with some very big questions: Who is in charge? Which group gets to have its way? Who should be our leaders and why? Throughout the years, we've developed a few basic systems that determine who gets to make certain decisions, but even with systems in place, the battle still rages.

Even in churches, most arguments arise because someone tries to control someone else. I once visited a church where the pastor seemed unusually tense. You could feel the tension in the air as he preached. At one point, he must have hit a really sensitive issue, because the organist struck a loud, dissonant chord on the organ, slammed the cover down, and stormed out. As she was leaving, the pastor yelled, "You are going to go to hell for this!"

That was a dramatic battle for control. It's not always that apparent, but there are lots of ways people grapple for it, and unfortunately, most of our small-group structures in church ministry today reflect that battle.

Often when I teach about free-market small groups, Christian leaders are tentative. They want to empower people, but not *that* much. They are concerned that people won't lead small groups the way they were trained or that they won't stay faithful to the vision of the pastor. They're afraid that someone might decide things are better another way, teaching ideas contrary to the pastor and leading them to leave the church. Training, expectations, loyalty, strict rules—these ideas are the ministry modus operandi for much of the leadership in the body of Christ. They often express themselves through systems that ensure that the people ministering in the church do it as the leadership would do it. Over the years, I have developed a different view of the "layperson."

Churches maintain influence over others the same way other organizations do. Some use the power of secrets, while others maintain their influence by simply knowing more than the other guy or by claiming moral superiority. All of us have seen people exercise authority over others by declaring God's authority over their lives, and certainly we see the standard chain-of-command system used all around us. Unfortunately, the system we see used when people are most desperate is old-fashioned force. All of these systems work in their own ways, and all of us operate in some of them to some extent every day. We have to. This is the way we establish order in our homes, our businesses, our communities, and our churches.

Much of the history of the world is the story of the struggle of human governance. This contest asks two questions: (1) What system, or combination of systems, do we use to maintain order? and (2) How much control over others is appropriate? Read books about wars, political upheavals, revolutions, and movements, and you will see six principal ways that people exert control: secrets, information, moral superiority, divine authority, chain of command, and brute force.

SIX METHODS OF CONTROL

1. Secrets

We've all seen situations in which someone knows something about someone else that would bring shame in that person's life if it were known publicly. Often in ministry we see leaders become privy to personal information that is private but, should the ministry go awry, is sometimes used to manipulate others. This is why the law protects the church from having to report illegal activity. The law recognizes that the church has to be able to communicate candidly with people in order for them to receive the healing that the church offers. At the same time, though, the power of secrets can be wielded by church leadership so as to hang over the people like the proverbial sword of Damocles—a haunting, ever-present dark cloud of reality over those who have secrets in their lives that they don't want exposed.

2. Information

When we go to a doctor or hire an attorney, we are paying the professional for information he or she has that might be helpful to us. The doctor or attorney has control over particular moments in our lives because he or she knows certain things we don't, and we have to trust that authority's judgment. Every business executive knows he or she can't make good decisions without accurate information, and often wars are won simply because one side has better information than the other. When people have information that others want, they can hold influence over those people.

President George Bush runs his administration this way. He possesses a powerful cadre of raw intellect in those he has placed around himself, his Cabinet. Being fully aware of each of the team members' capabilities, President Bush wields the experience, knowledge, and abilities of his team so as to create a power structure that has, as of this writing, moved American power, influence, and prestige to a level it hasn't enjoyed anytime prior to this.

One reason President Bush is successful is because he knows how to collect and to utilize information. Information and the effective use of it *is* power. David Kennedy, professor of American history at Stanford University, while positively noting Bush's success, said, "I give him very high marks for his remarks to Congress on September 20 [2001]. It was a very effective speech: measured, concrete, and moving. It did all the work that a speech like that has to do."[1]

President Bush's ability to use information powerfully—winning the public trust and trusting his advisors—was validated by David McCullough, author of *John Adams & Truman*, when he said,

> How in the world could George W. Bush have ever known that he would have to face the worst day in our history or that we would see in him the kind of vitality and crispness—of prose and decision—that he's demonstrated? He has risen to the occasion about as well as any public servant ever has. He's not afraid to express very fundamental, heartfelt, almost inexplicable devotions, devotion to country, devotion to God, devotion to old verities.[2]

3. Moral Superiority

Martin Luther King Jr. and Mahatma Gandhi prevailed in their struggles for freedom not because of superior military might or covert intelligence, but because they were right. They had moral vision that eventually won over their opponents. Sometimes a person is respected until some sinister fact about his or her personal life weakens that person's public position. Think of spiritual leaders whom we've all respected until a major failure occurred in their moral lives. Afterward, people who would never have had authority are suddenly able to impose their wills on the situation because they are deemed morally superior.

Bible authors employ this measure to gain influence with those to whom they are writing. To the early New Testament church the apostle Peter wrote, "I have written to you briefly, encouraging you and testifying that this is the true grace of God. Stand fast in it" (1 Peter 5:12). "My message is really *it*," he implied, "the absolute truth, so listen to me!"

It was his moral superiority that gave Paul his influence over the churches he founded and encouraged:

> When I came to you, brothers, I did not come with eloquence or superior wisdom as I proclaimed to you the testimony about God. For I resolved to know nothing while I was with you except Jesus Christ and him crucified. I came to you in weakness and fear, and with much trembling. My message and my preaching were not with wise and persuasive words, but with a

demonstration of the Spirit's power, so that your faith might not rest on men's wisdom, but on God's power. (1 Cor. 2:1–5)

"It is not I, weak and fearful, to whom you should defer," he was saying, "but my message—it is the very power of God!" Paul confronted the Corinthians not with his own superiority, but that of his message. In effect he played the "God card," challenging the people either to acknowledge or reject the moral superiority of his message.

4. Divine Authority

The Lord has given spiritual authority to men and women of God, and genuinely godly institutions reflect this authority. Because of this, pastors, teachers, overseers, bishops, missionaries, and those who are honest representations of God's authority are due respect, honor, and obedience to the wisdom they offer. Because of the power and influence God gives to those who carry His name, the Bible strongly warns against abusing this authority. However, we still find abuse. Some abuse authority by not understanding spiritual authority, and thus not submitting to or honoring those genuinely in authority over them—the very ones who could coach them in life if they understood spiritual authority. Others abuse it by using its power to manipulate and control people in an ungodly way.

5. Chain of Command

Chain-of-command control varies depending on each organization. If the right people are in the right positions of leadership, then there's little trouble. But sometimes people gain higher positions in the chain of command because of favoritism, family ties, or just good old-fashioned jockeying for position. The chain is sometimes too strong for people to get their jobs done: By the time they work their way up the chain, the issues they were working on have been exacerbated or have become irrelevant. Still the chain of command has its role—it is useful in helping people understand their individual roles and responsibilities, and it is critical to the functioning of institutions that depend on strict discipline for their success.

No institution has better utilized—and thus better exemplifies—chain of command than the United States Armed Forces. From the greenest private to the most battle-hardened sergeant to the most admired general, all know the importance of the chain of command and their own places and roles in it. From the ground to the air to the sea, subordinates hear and enact the orders of superiors for no other reason than the rank on each one's collar. This successful implementation of the concept of systematic influence by chain of command has helped established America's singular global military dominance.

6. *Brute Force*

If I have more guns, or if I am simply bigger than my opponent, then I will probably be able to get my way. Recently, the Taliban lost its last few cities in Afghanistan as the United States and its coalition of antiterrorist nations removed them from power. Obviously, the Taliban didn't want to give up Afghanistan, but our military might ensured that their opinion didn't matter. We had our way by brute force.

This is perhaps the oldest, most arcane system of power. Cain thusly foisted his will upon his brother; Babylon so influenced the course of Israel's events; and Rome built its empire this way. In the wake of the American Revolution, Alexander Hamilton and a few others published *The Federalist Papers* to persuade Americans to ratify the newly drafted Constitution. Wrote Hamilton of Great Britain's wielding of this power ax: "The world may politically, as well as geographically, be divided into four parts, each having a distinct set of interests. Unhappily for the other three, Europe by her arms and by her negotiations, by force and by fraud has, in different degrees, extended her dominion over them all."[3]

Throughout history, people and nations have amassed influence over others by the sheer exertion of superior force.

While we rarely see brute force used in church ministry, the other methods of control are employed regularly. These constructs are everywhere, used every day, cloaked in the visages of a thousand confirmation services and committee proceedings and catechistic dogmas. They live and they thrive and they largely determine the way things happen, from church picnics to global evangelization. Even so, Jesus taught a different method of gaining influence, a method far superior to the others.

Jesus taught that God would humble those who exalted themselves and that He would exalt the humble. He showed that the best way to have real influence in people's lives is by serving them. His model of service dramatically impacted the world as the church carried His example of humility to every nation and employed it to care for the poor, to treat the sick, to educate children, and to house orphans. Everywhere the church has been, benevolent organizations have been formed to provide a better life for common people.

The church is at its finest when it is serving people, and it always finds itself in trouble when it tries to use its influence to gain authority over people. As people of faith, if we're given any authority, we need to use it to serve others. When we have authority, we use it for the good of those who are within our influence, not our own good.

Please understand, I am not commenting on any particular church polity here. I am, instead, advocating that any form of, or system for, church governance should be used to serve and to protect those within its influence. I believe in the proper use of all of these forms of government. Likewise, I believe that each of them has an appropriate role, time, and place in serving others. On the other hand, each of them can be used to abuse those within their charge. I am being an apologist here for using church authority well—to provide the framework for great ministry within the congregation.

As an example, the Bible says that the husband is the head of the wife just as Christ is the head of the church (1 Cor. 11:3). What does this mean? Jesus provides for the church, loves the church, cares for the church, prays for the church, and protects the church. Thus, husbands are to provide for their wives, love their wives, care for their wives, pray for their wives, and protect their wives. Some husbands have thought about this from the paradigm of the first six sources of power, but Scripture is clear that it was because Jesus humbled Himself to the point of death on the cross that God exalted Him to the right hand of God the Father and made Him head over everything. Just as Jesus humbled Himself, so husbands are to humble themselves. Just as Jesus used His strength to serve the church, so husbands are to use their strength to serve their wives. Just as Jesus gave Himself for the church, so the Christian husband is to give himself for his wife. Some say that because Jesus is in charge of the church, husbands are in charge of their wives. But to be in authority over people is to be in a greater position of service to them.

So we know we need to do all we can to serve more and more people. In the first six methods, success comes from climbing on top of other people. In the Christian model, success comes from serving more and more people. Thus, if we find ways to serve people, then we are working in Christ's model.

Unfortunately, this servant attitude is poorly reflected in some of our church leadership. Go to a deacons meeting. Go to a church counsel meeting. Watch the power struggle between the board of elders and the pastor's office. "You know I give a significant amount of money to this church," people will say. Or "I've been in this church longer than you have been alive." What are they doing? They are trying to give a basis for why their opinions should win. Whew! What a battle.

We have to work within a combination of the six authority systems I've mentioned, but we as Christians have an opportunity to empower those systems with goodness when we use them with a servant's attitude. If we use the confidential things we know about people to make them feel secure, then we can use our power to serve. If we know more than others because of a stronger education, we can serve others with that information instead of lording over them. If we find ourselves in a position of moral superiority over others, we can serve them, and certainly if we have divine authority over others, it is given to serve. Chain of command can be used to serve those under our authority, and as in the example of the United States and its allies rescuing Afghanistan from the Taliban, we are using brute force to serve others. All of these systems can be used to serve, or to inflict pain, suffering, and tyranny. The world teaches us to control and manipulate with them. Jesus teaches us to use them to serve others.

THE MODEL OF FREE GOVERNMENT AND MARKETS

When the United States of America was formed, we called our elected officials public *servants*.

When people join our military, they come home and exclaim to their parents, "I just joined the *service*."

When Christians go to church, they say they have been to the *service*.

On our police cars, we print the words, "To protect and to *serve*."

In keeping with Jesus' example, we have defined the role of our political leaders as servants, and made them accountable to the very citizens they govern. We've organized our military and police forces so they have an elected civilian as their supreme authority, and we've given freedom from state control to our churches so they are forced to serve the public in order to survive. Our government is established "by and for the people" because we have a high view of the individual. "There is no form of government," said Benjamin Franklin, "but what may be a blessing to the people if well administered." America views the government's role as to serve—to "be a blessing" to—its citizens. We understand that people are the best judges of their efforts the majority of the time. We believe that individuals have the wisdom to select their own form of government and decide who fulfills the positions in that government. That is why we allow citizens to vote for a seemingly endless number of positions, to amend our constitution, and to decide various ballot issues each election year.

No one grasped—and believed—this principle of public service more wholly than George Washington. On the day he was notified that he had been chosen for the office of commander in chief of the American colonies' armed forces, Washington addressed the Continental Congress. His view of national leadership prompted him even to refuse pay for the service to which he had been called: "As to pay," he said, "I beg leave to say that no amount of money could tempt me to undertake this difficult work. I have no wish to make any profit from it."[4]

Washington was later elected president. The nation's first inaugural address captured stirringly the notion that he took office for the specific and singular reason of serving the American people. Spoke Washington:

> When I was first honored with a call into the Service of my Country, then on the eve of an arduous struggle for its liberties, the light in which I contemplated my duty required that I should renounce every pecuniary compensation. From this resolution I have in no instance departed. And being still under the impressions which produced it, I must decline as inapplicable to myself [any salary].[5]

Because we believe in the dignity of the individual, we in America elect our peers to write the laws that govern us, we elect the judges who oversee our courts, and we sit on juries so citizens cannot be prosecuted by the state before a panel of peers decides whether the law should apply. Without a belief in the dignity of the individual citizen, we would not have the Bill of Rights, the system of checks and balances, and the ability of citizens to petition the government. Essential to government as we know it is the idea that each individual has dignity, so the government works to serve each individual.

Just as we've organized our government so that service is rewarded and tyranny is forbidden, we've also organized our economy so that the consumer is served by being the one who determines which companies are successful and which fail.

In our free-market economy, businesses have to convince people that they are providing a product or service that is valuable. No business is done unless it is good for both the buyer and seller, and those values are to be determined by the buyer and seller themselves. Since we believe that individuals fundamentally know what's best for themselves, we give them the freedom to set prices by their willingness to buy a service or product at a certain price. If the price is raised above the value it offers to the individual consumer, then it is left unsold, which means that the price must be lowered in order to conduct business.

As long as Marriott is competing with Hyatt for the business travelers of the world, prices will be set freely by businesspeople. If, however, there were no competition, then the sole company providing the service would be able to charge whatever price it liked—and provide whatever level of service it liked—regardless of the consumer's desires. Since we believe that consumers need to be able to choose, we provide an environment that allows for several producers of the same goods and services to be available to the consumer. In short, we create a free market.

No recent American leader has embraced these big ideas of government for the people, the value of the individual, and the necessity of free markets and articulated them as clearly and passionately as the great patriot Ronald Reagan:

> What the world needs now is more Americans. The U.S. is the first nation on Earth deliberately dedicated to letting people choose what they want and giving them a chance to get it. For all its terrible faults . . . America is still the last, best hope of mankind, because it spells out so vividly the kind of happiness which most people actually want, regardless of what they are told they ought to want.[6]

For a more in-depth discussion on globalization, I recommend *The Lexus and the Olive Tree: Understanding Globalization* by Thomas Friedman (New York, N.Y.: Random House, 1999).

SO . . . WHAT DOES THIS HAVE TO DO WITH SMALL GROUPS?

Every free-market society currently in existence is based largely, to one degree or another, upon the principles I have discussed in this chapter. As a result, the people of these cultures have been trained and educated to think and behave based upon these principles. Yet many small-group systems have not respected the dignity and desires of the individual. Those who are responsible for them very often control them too tightly. They think they can dictate to average people what to think, what to study, and how to be discipled. Many of the small-group systems being tried haven't worked anywhere in the world because they disrespect individuals, don't give any room for innovation or creativity, and end up producing exactly what the old, top-down, heavy-handed military dictatorships, like the USSR, produced.

Think about it: the USSR had a politburo that dictated to people what to believe, where to work, how much education to receive, and where to live. As a result, they always had shortages or surpluses. The people lived in drab buildings, wore drab clothes, and were sentenced to a drab life in order to serve "the common good." The leaders claimed that this was a worker's paradise, but it wasn't. It seemed logical that this system would work, but it didn't.

Why? Because human beings are not machines. They each have a spirit that needs to be able to shine and to experiment. Human beings love to create and reach for the stars. They are inventive, thoughtful, and giving toward others. When a human being is in the right environment, he will shine in his concern for others. When in the wrong environment, he will become lazy and apathetic or too jaded to try to plug into another controlling system. In a worst-case scenario, the terror that can be unleashed from the heart of a human seeking control is unspeakable.

We have to ensure that our churches are not dictatorships run by politburos thwarting creativity and harshly dictating to people. We must be certain we're not restricting people's ability to soar. It's OK for people to try—which may lead to success, and it may lead to failure. Either is better than tyranny. If we don't take the risk, we might just get the same results as the USSR: unhappy people willing to risk their own lives to find some freedom.

In America, shopkeepers know that if people want something bad enough, they will pay for it. So in the summer when watermelons are plentiful, they are cheaper. In the winter when watermelons are scarcer, they are more expensive. In the summer, the fact that they are cheap sends a signal to watermelon growers that they will only get a certain price per watermelon, so they produce appropriately. In the winter, watermelon patches in other parts of the world know that watermelons will bring a higher price per watermelon, which makes it worth it to them to grow the watermelons and ship them to you. Thus, you have watermelons year-round. If the government either set the price of watermelons or mandated the production of watermelons, there would automatically be either a shortage or overabundance of watermelons. There is simply no way for the government to replace the perfect balance that the free market provides in the production of anything—watermelons, Cheerios, or Chevrolets.

It works the same way in our churches. If the government of a church says that it needs X number of small groups teaching subject Y, then you can count on it: Soon the pastor will either be announcing that there are not enough of the classes or that there are too many classes available and that more people should sign up to attend. I've been in churches where a central command determines which topics should be discussed, who should attend, and in what sequence they should attend. Some people comply, but most of those cooperate very reluctantly. They assume that the church leadership has their best interests at heart. But after time, people get tired of doing things that don't interest them, and they start demanding ministry that relates to them. Either the church allows this innovation, or it squelches it. Many small-group systems treat small groups like medicine: It tastes bad, but it's good for you.

But command systems do work. One I am closely familiar with succeeds because its administrators have established an elaborate method of feedback in order to continually adjust the services being offered to the congregation. They took away the market signals that we use through a rigid chain-of-command system, but they replaced them with survey after survey, so the leadership always knows the heart of the people. Most churches, though, don't survey their people continually, which means they end up just doing whatever they think is best. In essence, guessing.

In a free-market arrangement, the church government sets up systems so that people can establish whatever ministry they think others might be interested in. If lots of people attend and it meets their needs, others are free to start similar ministries. The market creates more and more so the supply meets the demand. If, however, the idea doesn't appeal to people, then those who were going to offer that ministry choose another ministry that will more effectively meet the needs of people, and both the people and the one offering ministry are more productive for the kingdom of God.

Free-market small groups make those who want to do ministry more fruitful and cause the correct amount of ministry to be available to the church without a shortage or surplus. As a result, the pastor doesn't have to coax people to attend, because the subjects offered match the wants and needs of the people. Nor does the pastor have to beg people to lead, because the people of the church will be deciding for themselves what kinds of things they want to offer to make other people's lives better.

What pastor would think of a mean-women's small group? No responsible one would. But it could be that the ladies of the church know that there is a need. What pastor would think of a prayer small group for Israel? Lots of them would. But if the pastor coaxed people to attend, it might end up making people unhappy that they committed to a small group on prayer that really doesn't interest them. (Buyer's remorse!)

We have 130 prayer groups in our church. They are popular because of the leadership and passion, and the demand for them comes from within the congregation. Just the fact that we have this much effort to pray for our church, our community, our nation, and other unreached nations has encouraged me to know that we can trust our faithful church members to do what needs to be done. I did not specifically ask for these groups to form—they formed out of the hearts of people hungry for God. Some of them are better than others, and the people who attend determine whether a small group grows or dies. Both directions are good. For those who grow, additional groups like them are created. For those who die, the leaders retrain and offer a more effective small group the following semester. I don't have to beg, manipulate, or coerce people. I just provide a way for them to minister. The people of New Life decide if the ministry is valuable to them or not, and they vote with their attendance.

This is the primary lesson of the twentieth century. At its core, the twentieth century was a global struggle over central government with command economies or government by and for the people with free markets. Freely elected government with free markets won, hands down, and people all around the world are measurably better off for it.

We are wise to understand clearly why free markets create wealth, provide what people want and need, and allow people to find their maximum productions. When we understand the value that God places on people, and when we allow them to create and become innovative, their products and services far outreach the things we could produce from our offices by ourselves. The fact of the matter is that free-market systems will help us all build much stronger ministries within our churches. Winston Churchill said, "There is no limit to the ingenuity of man if it is properly applied under conditions of peace and justice." So c'mon . . . let's be smart and utilize it.

CHAPTER SEVEN

Building a Culture of Opportunity

BEFORE WE DEVELOPED FREE MARKET SMALL GROUPS, OUR CELL
system attracted two groups of people. One group was the A+ crowd. These
are the positives 2s and 3s on the Engel Scale. They were dedicated and had
chosen to follow the leadership of the church. When we did Sunday school,
they would teach. When we did short-term mission trips, they would travel.
Whatever direction the church took, these were the early adopters. They
were in for the whole ride, committed through thick and thin. They loved
the church, they tithed, and they participated in obedience to God and His
delegated authorities. These are the people who make churches work.

The other group that was attracted to our old system were the most
needy people. These folks struggled with their relationships across the
board. They lived from paycheck to paycheck, didn't keep the same jobs
very long, had trouble finding affordable housing, and regularly needed

assistance from the church and the community in a variety of ways. These congregants generally didn't accept the wisdom of others, didn't adhere to the leadership of the church, and were often easily offended—which is sometimes why they were in the positions they were. These type of people feel as if they are fighting the whole world and can't trust anyone. Certainly, they usually have reasons for these feelings, but frankly, these feelings make them high-maintenance people who are difficult to help. Note that I'm not talking about people with genuine needs—I'm talking about people who are *needy*—difficult and stubborn in their situations, and skilled at making others feel that they need constant help.

Our system didn't intentionally do this, but it placed A+ people with the needy people—the A+ people led the groups; the needy people attended. This sounds as though it should work, but for us it was catastrophic. The A+ people enjoyed one another, but the needy people required a great deal of care. There was nothing to balance the dynamic that was happening in the small groups because we weren't getting a diverse mix of people.

I'll never forget the Sunday one of the A+ people came up to me at church and said, "I loved this church until we started the cell group in our home. Since we've started, I realized how much time these people take. Pastor Ted, is this church made up of mentally weak people?"

I started laughing, and he laughed too, but I could tell that it was going to be just a matter of time before he would become too busy to continue his cell group. Sure enough, he continued for another year and then stopped. In the end when I asked him what he thought of the experience, he said that he and his wife had done a great deal of ministry, but there were too many weird people, and he was no longer comfortable having them in his home. I asked him if he had formed any lasting friendships from his group. He said that he knew many more people, but he wouldn't consider them friends. They were, at best, acquaintances, investments, challenges because they had become so dependent upon him and his wife.

As we tried to make cell ministry work, we had several meetings about how the most needy people were feeling as though the A+ people were lecturing them, and the A+ people were not looking forward to cell meetings because they didn't have friends there. When the leaders went out for an evening, they didn't take the people from their cell groups with them. They took people from work, other friends from church, or other couples with whom they felt naturally comfortable. Don't get me wrong. They loved ministry and loved the Lord, but they considered their cell meeting a night of work rather than a night of growth.

Three Segments of a Congregation

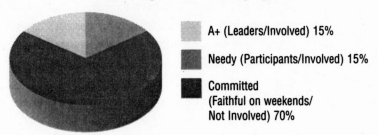

A+ (Leaders/Involved) 15%

Needy (Participants/Involved) 15%

Committed
(Faithful on weekends/
Not Involved) 70%

When we discovered that we were only attracting these two types of people, I began to pray that God would help us get, well, regular people—not just high achievers and low achievers, but regular folks too. I wanted the soccer moms, the accountants, the people who were just good Christians. Then I recognized the diversity of the people represented by the soccer moms, and I understood why many weren't attracted to our cells. They were extremely busy, and many already had a wide variety of interests, duties, and hobbies. I realized that they were doing great just to get to church on Sundays. Furthermore, they already had support teams around them with other moms in minivans driving from soccer practice to youth meetings. They all thought they should be attending one of our cell groups, but their schedules didn't allow for it, and in truth, our groups didn't appear attractive enough to make them shift one extra night a week.

I wanted everyone to come together. I wanted the A+ people to connect with needy people in a way that would be beneficial to both groups. And I wanted both of them to know soccer moms, accountants, college students, teenagers, young professionals, and so on. We needed to fill in the gaps.

It's clear to us now that our old system would never have allowed everyone to join our groups. It wouldn't even correctly serve either the A+ folks or the more needy individuals who came to it. We were creating the groups and telling people how to run them. The A+ people who could learn the system hopped aboard and supported it, but then burned out after some time—even those who faithfully continued to serve admitted it wasn't doing much for them. And the needy people came and went or just attached themselves to the stronger element, but couldn't figure out a way to genuinely serve the group or improve their own lives.

There were exceptions. They were the ones who formed genuine friendships within their groups, and they actually connected. When we saw this, we regretted that it was the exception rather than the rule. This motivated us to better understand the way people connect to ensure that a higher percentage of the people involved would find powerful connections with others. But certainly, the system we were using that seemed to be so popular with some wasn't working for the majority of our church, and it wasn't attracting any of our more loosely connected congregants.

The A+ people were doing the best they could with what we gave them. The needy people weren't being served and challenged in a way that helped them. And all the others just came on Sundays and got everything they thought they could from the church through the platform ministry. This is where we were during the time that we discovered our high backdoor rate, and the people who were leaving were the very soccer moms, college students, businesspeople, and retirees that we desperately needed to run our small groups.

LEARNING TO SAY "YES!"

One of the first basic issues that we recognized was that we hadn't yet learned to say "Yes!" We didn't know how to grant people permission to lead the kinds of groups *they* wanted to lead. Actually, we didn't even realize that they were waiting for permission. We didn't have a small-group culture that allowed for freedom of expression, opportunity, and creativity. Few of our A+ cell leaders tried anything unique in their groups because we never communicated to them that it was OK to do so. We expected them to host meetings that met the criteria we issued and to teach the materials that we were offering.

Albeit benevolently so, we found ourselves managing our small-group ministry in a way that was *permission withholding*. We held the power, the say-so, upstairs in our church offices, and we descended from on high to deliver unto the people the stone tablets of curriculum and policy for their groups. We tacitly communicated to our leaders through this system that permission to deviate in any way from the stone tablets was, by default, not granted. It was an understood and expected "no" in the same way as a child's request for a cookie before dinner. Any deviation, our system whispered, was by exception only, and should be kept quiet so as to preempt mass rebellion. We were permission withholding, and our people knew it.

They didn't feel free to cultivate their groups so as to facilitate friendships among members. They didn't feel free to adopt a subject for study that was of common interest (let alone to drop the study altogether and go fly-fishing!). They didn't feel free to let their group grow too big or stay too small or rotate its meeting place or deviate in any other way from the stone tablets. They didn't feel free. When people don't feel free, they do one of three things: They leave, become passive, or go underground. We saw some people do all of these things.

So when we made the philosophical jump and started to develop free-market small groups, we knew we had to find a way to transition from being permission *withholding* to being permission *granting*. A permission-granting organization is one whose default answer is "Yes." If there is a will, clichéd though it may be, there is a way. The role of the management is to find that way (and create it if necessary) which facilitates the entrepreneur's will. Where creative energy, ingenuity, and entrepreneurship are, there is progress. Where progress is, there is ownership. Where ownership is, there is a closed back door, and in time, there is growth.

Much has been made of the Nordstrom model. The department-store chain has distinguished itself in the business community because of its superior customer service, and justifiably so. Have you ever returned a pair of shoes to Nordstrom? It is a pleasure. You see, at Nordstrom, the answer is "Yes." The will of the customer—to do something unorthodox, perhaps, like exchange one shoe for a larger size—is valued by the company and is rewarded by the employee's finding a way. Easier? No. More efficient? Nope. More predictable? Not a chance. More *effective?* Absolutely, hands down, no question. Just go to Nordstrom and decide for yourself. I promise you, you'll keep shopping there too.

Another permission-granting company is Sears. A few months ago I sat in my living room and listened to my father-in-law recount with grand satisfaction the story of his experience returning a forty-nine-year-old Craftsman tool. "Lifetime means lifetime," he said simply, with all the sincerity of a man who had lived through the Great Depression but, as a modern consumer, still held to expectations of value. So in the back of his toolbox lay buried among other tools a defective socket for a socket wrench that he neglected to return. Decades after purchasing it, he walked up to the customer service counter at Sears and presented the defective socket. He told the customer service representative that he had purchased the tool in a set almost fifty years earlier, and that it had never worked properly. "This came with a lifetime warranty," he said plainly, in the same sincere tone with which he told us the story.

The customer service representative, who was younger than the tool by some ten years, responded politely, "You can pick out a replacement and bring it back to the counter." *Yes* was the answer, period. And now a third generation of our family is building things with Craftsman tools.

To be sure, permission granting is unsettling for management, unless management develops systems that are designed to serve a variety of people and needs. It's a risk to retire the rigid policy manual that so tidily produces and governs cell leaders. It'll make you feel a little out of control. But when you consider the alternative—to feel totally *in control* of a ship that might discourage some of your most innovative ministers—out of control holds a mysterious appeal. Really, it's not out of control at all. Actually, our small-group system is operating now in wonderful harmony. It's kind of like sitting in a lodge and watching skiers coming down the mountain. At first, the whole scene appears out of control—random and unintentional. It looks like chaos, and a collision seems imminent. In reality, though, everything is quite in control. Control is the norm, and to be out of control is actually illegal. The resort does not have to prescribe ski lanes or dictate a uniform ski pattern or style. All are free to ski as they please—one carves wide and slow across the whole width of the slope and another makes a bee-line of small, quick turns. Everybody is free of needless encumbrances and restraints, and everybody enjoys it more. This can happen because the resort has in place a set of parameters and safety regulations. As long as skiers stay within them, everyone is free and everyone is happy.

You see, when we replace our stone tablets and all the encumbrances they bring with *simple* and *clear* parameters and freedom to operate within them, we empower people. No more leader-bots—instead, men and women fulfilling their God-given ministry callings. I am convinced that leaders empowered to carry out *their* ministries, within the parameters of a healthy and stable local church, *are* the church's ministry. So in the same backward way that Jesus said the last shall be first, the more you decentralize, the more you accomplish. The more the people are fulfilling their ministry callings, the more you are fulfilling your ministry calling.

Yes, whatever it took, we knew we needed to jump the fence and force ourselves to be permission granting.

Recently ABC reporter John Stossel did a special in which he interviewed businesspeople who were trying to start their own businesses. The ethnicity, stage of life, and general skills of these people were all the same. The only difference between them was the country in which they were located. They were all Indians, but one group was in India, one was in the United States, and one was in Hong Kong.

In India, where there is poverty everywhere, people are starving and in need of basic services. Stossel explained that a businessman had purchased the rights to put a Kentucky Fried Chicken franchise in the area, but the local government held the business applications for years out of concern of humanitarian issues with the chickens and whether or not chicken meat was good for people. While the government held up his application to provide food, people were literally starving in the streets.

Stossel also demonstrated how a business was willing to invest to provide electricity to the community, but the government had held the application up for years due to technicalities. While this happened, the people were living without electricity in their homes and small shops. Excessive government control stamped out innovation and actually kept people from eating and having electricity in their homes. Never mind entrepreneurship. Obviously, in this environment, attempting to start a business was a death wish. The government wasn't serving people to help them accomplish their ideas, but instead it was a permission-withholding agency whose job it was to find the problem with ideas and, in effect, to stop most of them.

In the U.S., of course, it was significantly easier to start a business. Stossel showed first-generation Indian families who would not have been permitted to start their own businesses in India, but had been encouraged to do so in the United States. They were earning a living for themselves and their families, providing goods and services in their communities, employing people, paying taxes, and actually creating wealth in their communities and for their own children.

By far, the easiest place to start a business was Hong Kong. A group of Indian immigrants went to an office, filled out an application, paid a small fee, and *voilà!* They had a business. The contrast between Hong Kong and the U.S. was as great as it was between the U.S. and India. The journey from the stifling, permission-withholding culture of India to the permission-granting, innovative culture of Hong Kong was startling—one country seemed permanently depressed; the other teemed with optimism. It was creating wealth everywhere, and there seemed to be no limit to what it could do.

If we give the people of our churches the tracks to run on and the permission to go ahead and be creative and innovative, they will produce an abundance of ministry. If we insist on keeping control of the ministries of the church in our central command office, we will thwart creativity and innovation and end up with dysfunctional systems and depressed people—a sort of poverty within our churches.

ONE WAY WE SAY "YES": EASY ENTRANCE INTO LEADERSHIP

In our old system, extensive training was required for leadership. We had the idea that we had to "screen people out" until we found ourselves begging people to be leaders. Then we realized that there were two philosophies of training. One is the model that says we need to thoroughly train people so they know everything they need to know before they begin. The other is the old apprenticeship system that lets people begin working at their current skill levels and shape them as they go. We finally decided to utilize both ideas. We knew we at least needed to give people a crash course before they began, but we wanted them to start ministry as quickly as possible too. We knew that they would best learn the more subtle lessons of Christian ministry in the midst of the situations that develop within any small group.

Now the first step towards becoming a small-group leader is to attend a four-hour Small-Group Leader's Orientation on a Sunday afternoon. We have developed a fun, exciting, and informative four-hour orientation session that presents our vision and philosophy of small-group ministry, the role of a leader as a pastor, and an interview/application process to be approved as a New Life Church small-group leader. I'll explain this in detail in the chapter titled, "Nuts and Bolts." Once a prospective new leader attends this orientation, completes the application process, and is approved by one of the small-group pastors, he or she meets with the respective section leader (ministry coach) and begins the small group. Our new leaders have plenty of opportunity in the course of their groups to meet with their leaders through leadership training meetings as well as one-on-one coaching, so training is ongoing, hands-on, and very effectual.

Why do we have such an easy entrance into ministry? Three reasons:

The first reason is *Theology 101*. In order for anyone to become a new creation in Christ and to receive the guarantee of eternal life, that person must have the Holy Spirit indwelling his or her life. And because of the atonement that Christ provided on the cross, every believer has a personal relationship with God. This is the basis of the doctrine of the priesthood of the believer, which is the foundation of the Protestant Reformation. Since every believer has a relationship with God and the counsel of the Holy Spirit within, then every believer has the potential to be an effective minister to others. Everyone who believes in Him is a representative of His. This opens the door to validate and value the ministry of every believer.

The second is *Economics 101*. If something costs less, people are more likely to try it. When opportunities to lead ministry cost people less, they are more inclined to attempt leadership. I know of some churches that have raised the bar so high for ministry that their people in the busiest stages of life won't have the time or the patience to jump through all the hoops. S's and C's are more likely to go through the long, thorough training, but the I's and D's would rather just go do their own thing rather than sit there forever trying to get permission to start. If you make it easy to lead, people will lead.

The third reason is *Government 101*. Private property and the ability to own an idea because of the patent office are the foundations of quality and innovation. Since I own our home, I maintain it, want it to look nice, and want to increase its value both for the sake of my community and for my family's financial future. In addition, I own the idea of free-market small groups. God gave me the idea, I implemented it in our church, and because of that, I want to make it available to as many churches as possible that would benefit from it. Because it's my idea, I have an affinity for it and a desire to help other churches discover its benefits.

The people in your church are the same way. Everyone in your church has an area of ownership or expertise that, if shared, will help the lives of others in the church. We want them to be able to do all they can with their areas of strength to encourage and train others. Some people want to learn fly-fishing; while others want to learn dog training. Some need to know more about the book of Romans, while others need financial planning advice. Some need help with their marriages, and others need help with their kids, the neighbors, or their bosses. There are people in your church who can coach others in each of these areas and hundreds more. So if the church leadership encourages them to go ahead and teach in the areas where they are already strong, they—and the entire church—will benefit. Our short orientation session encourages people to come up with their own ideas—we don't waste hours or weeks trying to train them on our curriculum. What's more, we no longer have to recruit leaders; they step up out of their own passion and enthusiasm.

Please understand me when I say that I am very much an advocate for calling leaders to a higher standard, and I am convinced that our leadership approval process achieves it. However, I'm not an advocate for creating unnecessary, prohibitive hurdles that discourage people from even trying.

TWO IDEALOGICAL CONTINUA— INDIVIDUAL VS. COMMUNITY AND FREEDOM VS. EQUALITY

There are two major philosophies about how to improve people's lives. One says that if we allow individuals to prosper, they will improve the community as a whole. The other says that we need to focus on the whole community at once so that each individual will be better off. It's important for all of us as church leaders to decide what we think about these philosophies, because if we don't know what produces a better life for people, we might find ourselves promoting ideas that don't actually help.

In the last century we've had both government leaders and church leaders advocate both of these ideas in extreme ways. It's easy to contrast the USSR, Cuba, and North Korea with the United States. Communism and much of socialism focus on the good of the group. Individuals are made to sacrifice to improve the well-being of the masses. Property and goods are held in community. The U.S. policy focuses on the belief that it is up to each individual to create a life for himself, and that all people at all stages in life have the capacity to create some level of success for themselves and opportunities for those around them.

Of course, these policies exist on a continuum. No healthy person believes that just because he's part of a community he loses his individuality. Likewise, no one says that individuals forgo the chance to be a part of a group. The trick is to find a way to encourage individuals while keeping the group in mind, but not focusing on the group so much as to lose sight of the individual. There is a balance to strike, no matter how you view these ideas. I believe the most effective balance is found by placing a strong emphasis on individual people.

Historically, the greatest way to improve the quality of life for the group has been to do everything possible for each individual. If students individually decide that they want to be excellent spellers, then the class as a whole has higher marks. If a group of people decide on their own that they want to continue their educations and improve their income-earning abilities, the overall educational level and average income for the community is increased.

I believe that I am responsible to get an education, employ people, pay my bills, build relationships, articulate ideas, and make life better for my family. My culture has always taught me that if I want something, I need to work for it. In my little world, I need to pay my way. I am responsible to work and pull my own weight, plus the weight of a few others, no matter what the economy does.

But my culture is also a Christian culture, which means it's not hyper-individualistic. I don't want to be separated from others. In fact, part of the reason I want to be prosperous is that I want to be able to provide for others who can't provide for themselves. I want to combine my resources with a big group so that we can have a greater impact for the good. This is the strongest case I have for the importance of maintaining a strong corporate body in the midst of a small-group culture at New Life Church. My culture teaches that we are to help others with what's been given to us, but we are never knowingly to place ourselves in a position to need help from others—not because we're proud, but because we're supposed to pull others up, never drag them down.

The contrast to this is a culture of hypercommunity. Too often, people who have strongly emphasized community inherently believe that individuals within the community are the victims of the community. If the community suffers, the individual suffers. If the community succeeds, every individual succeeds. In churches that promote this rhetoric, you'll hear a lot of talk about the community, the community center, government housing, government subsidies, and government training. The whole community deals with crime; the whole community tries to succeed at once.

But exactly who is the community? How do you make a whole community safe? My mission is to make individuals within the community safe one at a time. Then the whole community is better off. I lean toward the power of individual strength and personal responsibility—if individuals improve themselves, they benefit everyone around them.

Martin Luther King Jr. understood this difference. In his famous "I Have a Dream" speech, he said, "I dream that one day my little children will grow up in a world where they will not be judged by the color of their skin, but by the content of their character."

Dr. King was intimating that when we think of people as whites, blacks, women, men, Americans, Hispanics, etc., we do a disservice to their individuality and their own abilities to create and to provide. The content of each person's character is his own personal attributes. Every one of Dr. King's girls would have to decide on her own to develop personal character, as would every one of his hearers. He was pleading with his audience to let people grow in their personal strengths as individuals rather than stifle them in the mumbo jumbo of group speak.

If we want our churches to have a culture of opportunity, we have to provide a framework in which individuals can strengthen the group as a whole without the group's holding them back. People have to be encouraged and allowed to excel, to break out of the pack, to stand up and say something and see if people will rally to their voices. If we force everything to conform, dumb down, and fit into the mold established by the church board or the senior pastor's office, we will stifle the very power that would enable people to rise up and create success.

Anytime we allow individuals to succeed, it modifies our strong belief in the importance of equality. We as Christians value equality to the point that we've institutionalized equality into many of our local church ministries: equal opportunity to lead within a church, equal opportunity to receive assistance, and equal quality from group to group. In order to enforce equality, we have standardized training, testing, and evaluation standards.

Equality can never be totally unimportant to us as Christians, but there is a place where the philosophy of equality becomes counterproductive. In our government, we want equal treatment under the law and equal opportunity for education, but that's about where equality stops and freedom starts. We don't believe that everyone should drive the same car, live in the same type of home, and have the same type of television. We believe, of course, that all are free to drive, dwell in, and view whatever they please. We can still go to North Korea or some sections of Cuba to see where the jargon of equality in every area of life leads us—to equal poverty and to bland living standards.

Freedom says Chevy families don't have to drive a Ford even though they are not equal vehicles. I know this sounds elementary and maybe a little absurd, but understanding this idea continuum greatly impacts our small groups. Do we want leaders to have total freedom? Should all groups be exactly equal? Actually, we don't want either extreme, so at what point on the continuum between the two should we be?

Everyone who deals with issues of human governance has to decide where the equality should stop and freedom should begin.

Suppose I have one hundred dollars that I want to give away. If I believe in freedom, then that means I can give the money to anyone I choose, and one person will be a hundred dollars better off. Someone who believes in equality would argue that since I don't have enough money to give everyone a hundred dollars, then I would be cruel to give my money to just one person. This rationale, of course, denies anyone the ability to receive the money.

I often see this argument in various forms in centrally planned churches. John Doe wants to minister to people who need help formulating a family budget. The church concludes that John can't help everyone who needs this service, doesn't have a standard procedure by which to train additional workers, and thus, since he can't help everyone equally, he shouldn't be able to start his ministry. "If we can't do it for everyone, we shouldn't do it for anyone."

This philosophy masks itself under the banner of precedent setting. "If we say 'Yes' to John, which we want to do, how can we say 'No' to Mark tomorrow?" This is why every leader has to decide his position on the continuum between freedom and equality. Freedom would have you give as much or as little of your money away as you want. It's freedom, and that freedom is a blessing to those who give and receive and is inconsequential to all others. Freedom says John can teach his class and that it doesn't have anything to do with those who don't attend. If it's a good class, others will take it, help John improve it, and the community will end up the better for it.

These two major leadership continua have to be considered and our positions settled in thinking about releasing people in ministry within the church. Let the individuals create and become productive, and that will lead to prosperity for the entire community. And lean toward freedom rather than equality, letting freedom raise the standard of ministry throughout the entire church. Take the risk of believing in individuals. Allow people to be different from one another and achieve more than others. Once these decisions have been made, growth and success are in the future for your church and ministry.

EVERY INDIVIDUAL HAS THE ANSWER FOR THE GROUP

The solutions to every problem any individual has within our churches can be found in other individuals in the congregation. The issue is whether there is enough freedom to match those with the solutions with those in need. In any church you can find someone who understands how to have a great marriage, but is a poor student. There is another person in the church who is a very successful student, but is struggling in marriage. The pastor can't spend time with both people, but he can encourage them to get together and coach each other. If they form a relationship and help each other, the first one will learn to learn, and the second will learn to improve his marriage. Because both of these individuals were strengthened, the entire church community is stronger.

Often when people in our churches have problems, they can't find any solutions outside of those offered by the pastor or a carefully selected group of people. But what if someone else in the church has a better solution? How ungodly would it be of us to stifle that solution if it would genuinely improve the lives of others? I believe all the people in the congregation have areas of expertise or wisdom. The art of great pastoring is to connect those with strength in an area to those with weakness in that same area so that the strength in one modifies the weakness in the other and neither person fails.

New Life Church currently has more than 800 small groups with more than 8,000 people attending each week. We have a membership of 8,700 people, and are currently 12 percent above last year. I'm not stressed. I have time to spend with my wife and children, time for vacations, time to sit here and write this book without pressure, and time to relax. How is this possible? Because we have built a culture of opportunity within the church so those who want to minister to others are able to. I don't have to worry about micromanaging the church, because the people of the congregation are involved with wonderful ministries of their own. Instead of controlling them, we support them. We developed a permission-granting atmosphere rather than a permission-withholding atmosphere so that people could minister in the areas where they felt capable. We train them as they minister rather than forcing them to know all they'll need to know before they begin, and the whole system makes life much easier for me and for our entire staff.

Very busy people lead most of our eight hundred groups. They are parents, business owners, and students. The vast majority of them would have very busy lives even if they were not so highly involved with ministry through the church. Normally, most of them would say that they don't have time to be too involved at the church, but they are here because they want to be. No one has forced them. Leading small groups gives them a chance to minister to people in a powerful way, and most of them become more involved each year, not less.

It really can work. The individual people of your church really do have the answers. We just have to find a way to encourage them to flourish in those answers and share them with the group. How? Please read on . . .

CHAPTER EIGHT

Capitalizing on the Force of Freedom

APPLE COMPUTER, INC. RAN A VERY POPULAR ADVERTISING campaign a few years ago titled "Think Different." The concept was simple: Each ad featured a famous innovator who had an important impact on our culture, with the phrase "Think Different" appearing below the character. Some of the people featured have had a great impact on the way we think about medicine, technology, and social reform (Albert Einstein, Thomas Edison, and Martin Luther King Jr.). Some were pioneers (Amelia Earhart and Neil Armstrong). Others were fabulous entertainers (Charlie Chaplin and Jim Henson). The common denominator in all of them was that each enriched our experience of the world by developing radically new approaches or styles that forever changed his or her respective field.

Why were these people able to make a powerful impact on the world? Why were they able not only to think differently, but also to develop and communicate their ideas?

LET FREEDOM RING . . .

. . . from the heightening Alleghenies of Pennsylvania!

Let freedom ring from the snowcapped Rockies of Colorado!

Let freedom ring from the curvaceous peaks of California!

But not only that; let freedom ring from Stone Mountain of Georgia!

Let freedom ring from Lookout Mountain of Tennessee!

Let freedom ring from every hill and every molehill of Mississippi. From every mountainside, let freedom ring.[1]

The famous words of Dr. Martin Luther King Jr. resound and echo back the answer. All of Apple's innovators were able to have the influence they had because they found the freedom to create, to produce, to innovate—*to think differently*. Of course, someone like Dr. King had to fight for the freedom to influence people, but he fought because he understood that God had given him individual liberty even if society was oppressive. Dr. King spoke boldly because he believed that the world would eventually recognize that inalienable freedom. And to a great extent, his dreams were realized. Today African-Americans are free to pursue their dreams without the degree of civil oppression that King and his contemporaries faced, and society continues to flourish because of their important and valuable contributions.

Or consider Henry Ford. Today we think nothing of driving on paved streets in neighborhoods that are planned to account for our cars. We live in a car culture, and it's impossible for us to imagine what it would be like not to drive. Each year we spend countless hours going from one place to another in automobiles, and we've developed stereos, leather seats, air-conditioning, and cellular phones to make that time more comfortable and efficient. We take car travel for granted, but none of this even existed 150 years ago. Ford came along and thought differently about transportation, and he forever changed the world.

Ford also thought differently about production. If my fuel pump goes out, I can go to any mechanic in any garage, and he can spend an hour installing a new fuel pump exactly like the old one. This is because Ford designed his Model T with interchangeable parts so that an assembly line could produce hundreds of cars in a single day. If a part of one car was broken or missing, it could easily be replaced by finding the part's model number. This idea is obvious to us, but only because Henry Ford developed it, popularized it, and made it part of our culture.

What if someone had told Henry Ford he couldn't develop his Model T? What if he had lived in a country like the Taliban's Afghanistan, where progress is extinguished and stringent social norms are enforced? Someone might have said, "No, thank you, Henry. People should not drive those things. We've always ridden horses and buggies, and we'll always ride horses and buggies. We should not confuse things." Or what if he had lived under a tyrannical regime like Pol Pot's Cambodia, where the government controlled commerce, assigned people jobs, and eliminated the innovators? How different our culture would be if someone had told Ford not to mass-produce so that cars could be available to everyone.

What if someone had told Mother Teresa that women would never be allowed to serve the poor in Calcutta?

What if Thomas Edison had been convinced that the candle-making industry wouldn't let him design artificial light? What if he hadn't been free to experiment with new ideas?

Innovators shape the world we live in. Rudimentary to innovation—the force that has allowed people to try, fail, try, succeed, patent, systema-tize, produce, and market—is the freedom to invent, own, and then distribute. These innovators either lived in environments that gave them freedom to pursue their dreams, or they created liberating environments so that others could pursue dreams of their own. Said Dr. Martin Luther King Jr., "Man is man because he is free to operate within the framework of his destiny."

Of course, freedom is risky. Freedom has intrinsic power to produce, and what it produces will always challenge the status quo. Freedom of religion means that people can construct competing belief systems. Scientology wouldn't be practiced without freedom of religion. Freedom of the press means that publications can promote bad ideas as well as good ideas. Tabloid newspapers exist and thrive because of freedom of press. There is no utopia—a system that allows for innovation and creativity in their best expressions necessarily allows for them in their worst expressions, as well. But it's worth the bother. It's worth putting up with the bad to have access to—and indeed to have the opportunity to create—the good. Let people try! Let them fail or succeed. The New York Times will always be taken more seriously than the National Enquirer. The Bible will always sell more copies than The Anarchist Cookbook. Good ideas prevail when freedom prevails.

As I was writing earlier, my cell phone rang. It was my fourteen-year-old son wondering when I was coming home. We spoke long-distance with no fees because distance doesn't mean what it used to mean. When we finished talking, I spoke to my wife, Gayle, who wanted to check some dates with my schedule. I pulled out my PalmPilot, and we adjusted a couple of things; later I'll synchronize those changes with my laptop, and my secretary will receive those same changes in her scheduling program. With all of these tools, our time is more and more efficient, and life is easier for all of us.

How did we become so efficient? Freedom. Bill Gates had the freedom to develop the software I'm using right now, and his competitors have freedom to improve upon it. I'm writing today in a Marriott hotel room, and surrounding me are a Hilton, a Hyatt, and a Holiday Inn. All of them have the freedom either to treat their guests to good or poor service. I chose Marriott for this trip, but I could choose Holiday Inn for the next one. I have the freedom to choose, and the hotel chains have the freedom to solicit my choice. This culture of freedom virtually ensures that products and services will continually improve.

Freedom facilitates innovation. It makes the market work. It's the bulwark that undergirds the lifestyle we enjoy. It pushes civilization toward rapid advance. It makes democracy work. We are able to love the things we love—from Sunday worship to universities to shopping malls to high-school football—because most countries now recognize that they don't have the right to take them away from people. They are God-given. No police officers come to my house on Sunday morning to make sure I haven't gone to church. No one limits how much money I spend on lettuce or Twinkies. No one says I have to wear a certain type of shoe or drive a certain kind of car. No government agency proofread this text. Why? We live in a free country, and though most of us may take it for granted, it is freedom that shapes our lives.

FREEDOM VS. CONTROL

But what about our churches? Are we getting the full benefits of freedom?

Every church should ask itself whether or not it encourages its people to minister to others in new ways. Are we creating and embracing change, or are we tentative about it? Does the church encourage creativity or stifle it? No doubt, in the last thirty years, many churches have improved at lightning speed, and it's easy to see which ones create and embrace innovation. But unfortunately, many constrain improvement because it pushes us out of our comfort zone for a time. Is a car better than a horse? We weren't certain at first. Is a computer better than a typewriter? ("What's a typewriter?" some of you might ask. Hmmm. That was a fast switch!) When weak computers consumed entire buildings and didn't work well, many were sure there was not much use for them. No doubt, change is not always improvement. But unless we take the risk of change, we can't find the ideas that will create improvements.

Risk? This is what everyone fears. What about bad ideas? What about people with poor character? What about insubordination? What about failure? Church splits? Gossip? Uneasy nights? Hatred? Nope, it's not worth it.

We all want innovation—as long as we are the idea people and we are persuading others. It is comparatively more unsettling to let others innovate. Certainly, on the one hand we all want to be more effective at ministry. On the other hand, taking the risk within our own proven ministry systems to allow for a bright idea that might reach a new group of people might threaten what we've already built. But if we protect what we've already built with the methodologies that we've always used, will we just continue to produce what we've already produced without improvements? I know. It makes us all uncomfortable. Since we know that everyone has some type of ministry calling, though, we had better reform our structures to allow believers to try the ministries that God has placed within them or we might miss the computer, the cellular phone, and the automobile.

But risk seems so taxing! Is it true that we have to take the risk of building the systems that empower and strengthen people to do what they are called to do? It is so much easier to have a handful of well-trained, trusted ministers to serve the congregation. I agree, but evidence suggests that we're missing some of our greatest potential by taking the easy route. Some of our best ministers have had to step outside the structure of the local church to do ministry. It's incredible to think that we actually have church-governing systems maintaining the status quo rather than providing a safe place for Christians to take risks in an environment of flexibility, creativity, development, change, and improvement. The same can be said of some parachurch ministries. Too many are ruled by a resistance to change rather than a culture of freedom, which unfortunately means that the best ideas are often lost.

Many churches do a good job of teaching about the power of the Holy Spirit. If we genuinely encourage people to be filled with the Holy Spirit, though, we had better be prepared for the work that He will do in them. You see, the Holy Spirit is in the business of change. He is Mr. Change; it is what He does, and He does it well. He comes into people's lives and starts changing them, and as this process develops, He starts giving them ideas for change. The Holy Spirit is the Spirit of Creation. In a fallen world, He always creates change because He is the agent God uses to make the world a better place. Thus, He always improves things. He always rearranges our furniture. He always adjusts the status quo. So when He fills His people, we all prosper if our structures facilitate change. But if our structures constrain change, it's just a matter of time before something breaks.

In civilized countries, people are accustomed to having the freedom to do what they believe is best for themselves and those around them. Consequently, when the church gives responsible people freedom, they know how to make the most of it. Most of the believers around us buy their own stocks, start their own companies, design their own homes, and plan their own schedules. I'm not questioning the importance of the rules and parameters within which each of these functions must be performed; I am saying the role of the structure is to facilitate the safe and constructive execution of their design. Some may feel thwarted, but most people are wise enough to know how to do what they can with the wisdom and strength of the structure that empowers them. This is the mentality and worldview that our churches can now use to the fullest.

The free-market culture I described earlier is apparent everywhere, and people justifiably resent unnecessary controls. Many churches are catching on to this and are shifting their ministry training from top-down, rigid, chain-of-command styles that are characteristic of the old mainline and/or liberal denominations, to independent networks that are more fluid and can freely strategize together and incorporate the best new ideas. Many of the new apostolic networks and modern parachurch phenomena like Youth With A Mission are doing this well. The Southern

Baptist Convention and the Evangelical Free Church of America are two networks of churches that have benefited from the flexibility they allow among their network of churches. Innovation is improving the way we do church just as Microsoft, AT&T, and AOL are changing the way the world communicates. All of these organizations have order, a chain of command, and a strong hierarchy. But they use their authority to provide an environment for innovation.

Of course, every one of us in leadership has to decide how much freedom is appropriate. No thinking person believes that total freedom is wise. Every relationship restricts freedom. Every responsibility restricts freedom. When we marry, we voluntarily limit our own freedom in order to build a trustworthy relationship. As we have children and advance in our careers, our freedoms are constrained to take on those new responsibilities. Every police officer knows about restricting people in order to protect the freedom and safety of others. There is a balance between absolute freedom and absolute control. The trick is to grant as much freedom as possible while maintaining a responsible civilization.

In the United States, the first four presidents were in constant tension as the meaning of our nation was being defined. George Washington and John Adams were Federalists who believed that government should be elected by and for the people, but that once elected, governments should exercise considerable strength. Thomas Jefferson and James Madison felt that it was the role of the elected to ensure that government did not restrict the lives of its citizens. This same argument continues to this day in the philosophical struggle between the Democratic and Republican parties. The Democrats have a fundamental belief in the positive role the government can play in the lives of people, while the Republicans insist that people do better when left alone to take care of themselves. Democrats emphasize the responsibility of the group, while Republicans emphasize the responsibility of the individual. This healthy tension continues as we work to discover how much freedom is appropriate.

The battle rages in the church too. How much should the church government control what the people in the church are studying? How much should the church control who teaches? How much should the church control where and how members meet? How much should the church dictate the style of ministry?

I maintain that the best way to facilitate maximum creativity and growth is to allow as much freedom as possible. Tip the scale toward freedom. As I said, freedom is risky. Giving permission means mistakes will occur—no way around it. Inevitably, ideas will creep up that we don't like, some of which might even be dangerous. We've got to deal with them and sort through the bad ideas to find the good ones. Undoubtedly, it can get messy, but it's better to deal with the mess than not to have any new ideas to deal with at all.

Several will strike out before we get a home run. But the people in our churches are sharp, God-fearing people who have been blessed with considerable gifts. If we respect and appreciate them, the freedom to try new ideas will reward all of us. When they succeed, we'll applaud them and empower them even further. When they fail, we'll coach them and help them try again. Either way, we win.

MANAGING A CULTURE OF FREEDOM

A train can't run without tracks. In a church where freedom is a strong value, we need guidelines to direct us. How do we know for sure when to constrain someone's freedom when it comes to, for example, teaching the Bible? How do we ensure that our Sunday school teachers and small-group leaders can be both creative and responsible in their teaching? How can we harness the strength of individuals so that it will strengthen the whole community of believers rather than tearing it apart? My starting point is to understand the difference between absolutes, interpretations, deductions, and personal/cultural preferences.

Absolutes

Absolutes are the essentials of our faith. The existence of God, the integrity of Scripture, the death and resurrection of Christ, and the reality of heaven and hell are all absolutes. They are the foundation for everything else we believe. At New Life Church, our statement of faith reflects what we consider to be the absolutes, and in order for anyone to teach in our small groups, the candidate has to be willing to communicate our statement of faith. If one is not willing to teach our statement, then he or she is not allowed to lead one of our small groups. So in regard to absolutes, leaders of our small groups have no freedom. They must be willing to teach them in order to have a role of authority in our church.

Interpretations

Our statement of faith doesn't cover everything. There are many areas of Scripture that are subject to interpretation that are not covered in our statement of faith. In these areas, our small-group leaders have greater freedom. For example, we currently have two groups each led by former college professors—both with Ph.D.'s—on the subject of creation, science, and the Bible. One group is called "Kids, Science, & the Bible." The leader has a desire to help parents of school children interpret some of the things their kids are taught in school about creation, and demonstrate how science fully supports the Bible. He believes in an "old earth" with a more recent appearance of mankind. In other words, a "day" in Genesis 1 could be a thousand or even a million years. The other group is called "Scientific Evidence of Creation." The leader of this group believes in a "young earth," or the seven literal twenty-four-hour days of creation. Both of these leaders are considered "creationists," both believe that the Scripture allows for both interpretations, and both shake hands and greet each other warmly on Sunday morning. Both groups are effectively discipling people, so rather than saying one is right and the other is wrong, our church offers both and lets the people decide which is best for them.

Another example is the variety of small groups that pray for Israel. Some of these groups believe that virtually everything Hebrew is divine. They celebrate Jewish festivals, wear Jewish shawls during prayer, and believe that every event in the Middle East points to the return of Christ. Other group members who pray for Israel do so because they believe that Israel is the only democracy in the Middle East, and it needs a protective prayer covering. They aren't as interested in end-times theology. Some people in our church love the focus of the first group I described; others love the second type. It doesn't make any difference to me. I see the value in both types, and think the two groups are reading the same Scriptures in two different ways. Neither group is heretical, so I can be relaxed with their freedom as long as they respect one another. Our small-group system provides the freedom for people to acknowledge Israel as they see fit.

Deductions

While an interpretation is explaining what a passage of Scripture means, a deduction is taking one verse from one place in the Bible, connecting it with a verse from another place, and then coming to a conclusion that would not be evident from either of the verses on its own. Or it's when we look at one aspect of culture, combine it with something else from culture or from Scripture, and draw a firm conclusion. Thus, a deduction is a construction, an equation that says A + B = C.

With deductions, managing freedom is a little trickier, because people can deduce all sorts of things. We have more than eight hundred students a week who attend our home-school enrichment small groups. Many of these students are being homeschooled because their parents have made a series of constructions from Scripture and culture that has led them to believe that the government school system is inappropriate. They want their students educated at home and at church, not by agents of the state.

I am sympathetic to this stream of thought, but I don't believe it myself. A few years ago I coauthored a book with John Bolin titled *Confident Parents, Exceptional Teens*[2] in which I encouraged Christian high-school students to attend government schools so they would be exposed to secular ways of thinking and temptations. I believe that it's best for students to encounter those things while they can still come home to their Christian parents and process what they're learning. But I know that my ideas are not right for every student, and neither are those of the home-school advocates. Thus, I'm an advocate for our home-school enrichment small groups, but I also defend the parents who keep their kids in public schools. I also understand the argument for putting kids in Christian schools, so I defend those parents too. People argue strongly for all sides here, but I say that we *should* let freedom ring for all approaches.

Personal/Cultural Preferences

Outside the three concentric circles of absolutes, interpretations, and deductions are personal preferences, feelings, and cultural norms. This is where we come into discussions about worship and prayer styles, music, clothes, and so on. It's in these areas where things like church small groups can really shine. I'm thankful for the large variety of tastes and interests represented in our congregation, because it creates a culture of diversity and opportunity.

Diagram of an Individual's Belief System

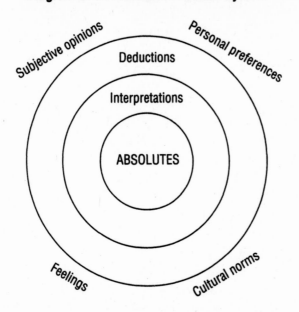

I hate fishing, but I am raising four boys who love to fish. The Prime Ministers (over-fifty crowd) of our church have a small group that is dedicated to taking the young men of our church fishing with them. As a result, my sons have a warm and friendly relationship with a group of the older members of our congregation because they have baited hooks and reeled in fish together.

Why am I excited about this? Because this is a ministry that sprang up out of the hearts of our older congregants, and it's an event that I would have never considered ministry. My boys had never been fishing with grandparents or uncles, but now they've had wonderful experiences fishing with men in their sixties, seventies, and eighties. They have prayed together with these men. They have sat around the campfire with them and listened to their conversations, and they have come home with deep admiration and respect for these people in our church. The fishing group has given my boys a clear picture of mature, godly manhood.

Now, if we had only ministries designed by the central command of our church leadership, we would have never known how to form a group of older people to take younger people in our congregation fishing. But when the older people have an idea, they can run with it, and it improves all of our lives. Freedom is the force that gives people the ability to create ministries that change people's lives.

TRUSTING OTHERS?

Oddly, Christians often fight against freedom in churches while fighting for freedom from the government. Christians provide the theological basis for human dignity and honor for all people. We are the ones who defend freedom of the press, freedom of religion, and freedom of speech all over the world. We don't think that government should have a role in dictating to its citizens how they should worship or think. We think business owners should be free to run their businesses and that people should be free to spend their own money. We don't like government imposition in any area of our lives.

So, we are philosophically on the side of freedom . . . until it comes to the management of our churches. Once inside the walls of our churches, we create dictatorships or politburos that dictate policy and thought. In some cases (thankfully not very many), we have the equivalent of military dictatorship, where dissenters are threatened with expulsion and hell. Please understand: I believe strongly in spiritual authority in the church. But I believe it's best if the church understands that it is in a place of influence and power in the lives of church members to mobilize them in their ministries. To make them effective. To empower them. To prepare them for the callings that are within them. We need to use our spiritual authority to equip others and provide an environment of freedom so they can blossom in effectiveness and bless other people.

So why doesn't every church do this? I think there are two reasons. One is because the leadership actually believes that it knows how the people in the congregation should influence and impact other people. Sometimes church leaders develop a kind of spiritual snobbery that causes them to believe that they know best, and that people should think and do just as they think and do. They're uncomfortable with variety and diversity.

Another reason is that church leaders are afraid that people will go their own ways. Their natural response is to employ a "one size fits all" style of ministry—believing that the only way to control things is by standardization. Regularly when I am teaching on the power of free-market small groups, people will ask me if we've had small groups break away from the church, leave the church, or become their own church. I respond by saying that the opposite is the case. We have the same problem as the United States and other free countries. We don't have difficulty with people trying to get out of our influence, but with people wanting to get in. Our issues are not with people wanting to leave and start their own church, but with people outside wanting to come into our system so they can fulfill the ministry God has called them to. Not a bad problem to have, eh? Our biggest concern is trying to figure out how to include everyone. It's wonderful!

It really is OK to give people freedom. They know how to handle it. When people are wisely empowered, they don't despise the leadership and try to undercut them. Rather, they submit to coaching and direction. They don't become subversive. They become genuine leaders and disciples, which is what we've wanted them to be all along. Freedom isn't dangerous, and it isn't complicated. It's the most powerful catalyst I know for good ideas, growth, and expanded ministry. It might feel a little scary to give people too much freedom at first, but once we do it and see the amazing fruit it produces, we'll become addicted to freedom, and the kingdom of God will produce and expand like never before.

CHAPTER NINE

Functional Discipleship

WHEN WE FOUNDED NEW LIFE CHURCH, ONE OF THE FIRST things we needed was a worship leader. There weren't too many worship leaders around who were willing to lead a tiny group of believers in the basement of our home, so for several weeks we just pulled out a little stereo and worshiped along with a tape. But before long, a brother came along who offered to help with worship. He was great—passionate, skilled at singing and playing guitar, and sensitive to the Spirit of God. We loved him, and the people of our growing little church loved worshiping with him.

But this brother had his share of problems. He was a chain-smoker, his clothes were disheveled, and he couldn't keep a job for more than a few weeks. He seemed so irresponsible in so many ways. Often I had to send someone over to his trailer to pick him up. Much to my embarrassment, he would often beg five or ten dollars off the person giving him the ride.

We tried to take care of him and help him get his life in order, but he was apparently comfortable the way he was and unwilling to change. He'd often step outside the basement door (which was our church) during the sermon to smoke, then come back in for the closing prayer. He loved praying with people, but as he prayed they'd be overcome by the smell of smoke on his breath.

As odd as it sounds, God seemed to bless this man's ministry. Our worship times were anointed, and he was great at leading people in prayer even if he did reek of smoke. Even though his hair went unwashed and his glasses were broken and held together with a paper clip, this brother had a kind heart toward people, a tenderness before God, and a loving and gentle spirit. He would never have met the requirements for leadership in a typical, well-organized megachurch. He must have met some of God's requirements, though, because God allowed him to lead worship honorably for our church for several years, even as we reached more than over a thousand people in regular attendance.

I'm happy that our current worship leader, Ross Parsley, has a nice haircut, tucks in his shirt for church, and doesn't smoke, spit, or chew tobacco. But I've never forgotten how important our first worship leader was to the growth and ministry of our church. He didn't fit the standards for a church staff position. But, there's no doubt in my mind that he was called by God for that season, and he ministered to a certain type of people who may have never set foot in our church otherwise.

Don't get me wrong. I'm not arguing for a lack of standards. Rather, I am contending that there is a role for just about everyone in the body of Christ. There's a mystery here that we need to grasp: *God chooses unlikely people and puts them in unlikely positions.* Think of the Virgin Mary. Here was an ordinary teenage Jewish girl, one minute going about the ordinary business of life, the next being visited by an angel of the Lord: "The angel went to her and said, 'Greetings, you who are highly favored! The Lord is with you.' Mary was greatly troubled at his words and wondered what kind of greeting this might be. But the angel said to her, 'Do not be afraid, Mary, you have found favor with God'" (Luke 1:28–30).

Sure, it all makes perfect sense now, in hindsight—the baby Jesus, born to the Virgin Mary, on a road trip, in a stable. But just try to imagine this scene from the perspective of the Jewish people who had been awaiting their Messiah—their Deliverer and their King—for several centuries. The patriarchs descended from Abraham, a man of great wealth and influence. Moses was raised in Pharaoh's house, the seat of international power in his time. And the Messiah was being born . . . to a *peasant girl?* Wait a minute now . . . *Where does she come from? What is her lineage? What is her training in the Torah? Does she keep the law? Who is this girl?*

Think of Saint Patrick. Here was an uneducated, barely articulate slave boy, stolen from his family by marauders as a young child, growing up alone on a hillside, tending livestock. No home. No family. Cold, brokenhearted, and alone. It was to this teenage boy that God chose to reveal Himself and to assign the awesome task of evangelizing the British Isles and much of the European continent. The unschooled, ineloquent, and presumably emotionally frazzled Patrick was God's agent to introduce civilization to barbarian Medieval Europe. Who would have thought?[1]

Yes, God has a way of choosing unlikely people for unlikely positions. Often His choices seem odd to our perspective, but they always fit together perfectly in the scheme of eternity. Our first worship leader was an unlikely candidate by any standard, but he drew people to church who would never have come to hear a twenty-eight-year-old, clean-cut Indiana farm boy. I drew people who were feisty and fun-loving, but conservative, with Midwestern core values. The variety of cultures is still the hallmark of New Life. Through our free-market small-group system and the variety of styles it encourages, our church feels comfortable to the farm boys, the ex-hippies, and everyone in between.

Everyone in our churches has the potential to be a life coach in someone else's life. Sometimes in Christian circles we get caught up in an attempt to train people to be certain types of leaders—to fit one particular mold or another. Of course, roles are important (such as the apostles, prophets, evangelists, pastors, and teachers that Paul mentions in Ephesians 4:11), and we need to continue to encourage people to flourish in their callings. But not every leader looks the same, and some leaders don't look like leaders at all—at least not according to our traditional models.

In our church, we have eight hundred small-group leaders, sixty-six elders, seven trustees, five overseers, eighteen pastors, dozens of ushers and support staff, and hundreds of volunteers. That's nearly a thousand different people with different shapes, sizes, interests, approaches, and techniques. The only thing we all have in common is that all of us are life coaches, responsible for learning how to help other people live life well (and for learning from others how to live our own lives well), and all of us are called under the banner of the same local church.

THE ELEMENTS OF DISCIPLESHIP

Here is my premise: You and the other people in your church are already discipling people. Influencing others doesn't just happen when we form special accountability or Bible-study groups. It's always happening—we take natural relationships and make them purposeful. Discipleship doesn't require going to a seminar or taking people through a booklet; it requires being intentional about helping the people around you right now to grow in their faith.

In the George Barna book I mentioned earlier, *Growing True Disciples*, he lists nine baseline elements of discipleship.[2] I love his list, so I'm going to walk you through it and show how each facet of discipleship occurs natu-rally within the free-market small-group system.

1. Passion

I believe that most people want to improve their lives, and they will do so if they can be in a comfortable environment. Free-market small groups give people the opportunity to take their heartfelt religious convictions and deal with them in an environment that is not only nonthreatening, but is the very environment in which they naturally place their passions. If people are passionate about movies, they can use that passion to meet with other people and talk about movies. If people are avid mountain bikers, they can bike with other people who are also passionate bikers. The free-market small-group situation has all the pleasure and comfort of a great parks-and-recreation club, plus a leader who is subtly or overtly (depending on each group member's place on the Engel Scale) discipling people toward God's perfect plan for their lives.

Rob Stennett is a college student in our church. He attends the University of Colorado, where he is an English major, and he also leads a small group here at New Life. Since he was a boy (I have had the pleasure of watching him grow up), Rob has always been passionate about books. Fantasy, mystery, science fiction, war—all of the great subjects of novels have always captivated him. Wherever I see him, he always has a book in his hand.

It was only natural when the time came for Rob to go to college that he would choose to study literature. Nobody was surprised, nor will anybody be when he teaches literature to high schoolers or college students one day. Do you know what Rob Stennett's small group is called? New Life Literary Society. Every two weeks, a dozen or so young people from our college group read a book and then gather to discuss it. Rob chooses the books, leads the discussion, intentionally incorporates Christian ideas, and disciples the members of his group. Our college pastor didn't have to twist his arm to get him to lead a small group—he simply had to give him the freedom to do what he was already passionate about.

As the senior pastor, the thing that I enjoy most is that I no longer have to motivate people to form small groups and disciple others. They are already excited about their groups because they're doing what they would naturally do anyway. All that the staff and I have to worry about is managing the blessing of so many people growing in their personal ministries.

2. Depth

There have been times when I've wondered if anyone was really listening to my sermons. I don't anymore. Why? Because with free-market small groups, my sermons are not just about delivering information; they are about the ministry that is going to go on through hundreds of people in the congregation each week. People listen because they want to be able to explain the ideas to the other people in their small groups.

I am an exegetical Bible teacher. I love teaching books of the Bible verse by verse. But depth of insight only happens only when the listeners know that they not only have to apply that teaching to their own lives, but also have to understand the material so they can apply it to the lives of the people whom they are responsible to coach. Thus, they don't nod off in church or watch the time restlessly. Instead, many of them pull out their notebooks and attentively take notes, wanting God to impart to them the wisdom of His Word so they can coach others.

3. Maturity

I'm always deeply disturbed when I meet a Bible teacher or Christian leader who hasn't learned how to handle jealousy, envy, or other personal issues. Bible knowledge and being able to wow a crowd are one thing; genuine

Christianity is another. Christianity is in the living, not just in the believing. Believing the facts of the gospel is not equal to being a Christian, and it's certainly not equal to being a Christian leader. Bible knowledge has got to be proved, refined, and developed in the midst of personal relationships. How we manage love, hate, affection, rejection, passion, and admiration reveals who we really are. Free-market small groups force the application of Scripture—the genuine knowledge of it—by ensuring that people are in relationships that hold them accountable to that application.

It has always interested me that all of the Old Testament prophets were unable to fully communicate the truth about God, so He had to come in person to demonstrate what He was like. He showed us His character through His relationships with a few fishermen, a couple of tax collectors, some Pharisees, a harlot, and a thief on a cross. The revelation of the divine by means of His incarnation in the form of a man is an incredible concept, and I think it continues today as the principal role of the body of Christ. We can't merely teach godliness; we have to embody godliness.

I believe God so insists on this idea that He won't allow His character to be ingrained into our lives without its being imparted and refined through relationships. The only way I know to develop character and integrity is in the midst of others. Can we be humble standing in a room by ourselves? I'm not sure, but I know I have to figure out how to be humble when I'm tempted to be arrogant toward another. Try to isolate yourself and be kind, patient, gentle, or selfless. Character is validated within the context of relationships.

The group instruction that we receive in church is valuable, but it has to be integrated into our lives with friends and enemies. And to be refined, it must be coached through regular meetings with friends. As Christians, we are transformed people, which means we have become transformed in the way we relate to others. That is the process of maturity.

4. Practice

Earlier today I received a phone call from one of my associate youth pastors who had just finished a tense meeting with an angry parent. The parent was upset because of the way her eighteen-year-old son had been handled in a recent ministry meeting. My associate did a fine job managing both the son and the parent, but I am sympathetic to the parent because I know the difficult situation her family faces.

Circumstances like this always make me thankful. I much prefer a thoughtful call from a parent to no communication at all, knowing all too well the slippery slope silence can create. Because the parent was wise enough to initiate the conversation, we can all think through this together. In the next several days and weeks, the parent, the son, the youth pastor, and I will all be praying, talking, and thinking about the right thing to do, and we'll all end up growing in Christ.

See why this is so important? Working out godliness is a mix of biblical principles, family passion, strained relationships, terrible mistakes, grace, church structures, and awkward confrontations. No one likes to go through these processes, but we're all better for it in the end. Feelings may be hurt, but they will be healed. And when this situation is smoothed over, the family will fondly remember the youth pastor for the rest of their lives. I've seen it happen over and over again. Now *that's* discipleship.

5. Process

In our lives as Christians, we are running a marathon, not a sprint. Discipleship is a process, not just a series of classes that we can complete and then conclude that we have been discipled. I jokingly say that the reason we have children is to force all of us to grow up. Children force their parents to live for others, be patient, think long-term, seek the grace of God, and be wise. As parents come to me while learning these lessons in their thirties and forties, I can only imagine these same people in their late teens or early twenties explaining to their parents that they are adults and don't need to be told what to do. (Right. We know.)

The sure way to identify a baby Christian is to listen to him boast about his understanding. The problem with growing up is the same as the problem with maturing in Christ: It's a process that regularly deceives us. We keep thinking we're approaching the finish line, only to discover that there's another starting line. As we grow, we learn how much more we need to develop in Him. It's like a man exploring an iceberg. He sees only the tip poking out of the water and wonders what's below the surface. As he begins to explore, he finds there is far more under the surface, and so the process goes. The more he sees, the more he understands how little of the whole iceberg he has actually seen.

Thus the importance of free-market small groups. We are in a lifelong process, and no one curriculum, teaching series, or teacher can competently walk any one of us, much less a large, diverse group of us, into maturity in Christ. We need variety, diversity, and a multiplicity of gifts, personalities, and experiences. Only such diversity can hope to address the complexity of the discipleship process. Free-market groups are necessary in a church for the same reason that we probably shouldn't get our graduate degrees from the same school where we did our undergraduate work. Or better yet, we would never think of getting our bachelor's degrees from a high school, or getting our high-school diplomas from an elementary school. Each level of school is important, but one is not sufficient on its own. We need variety, diversity, and new challenges.

People in their seventies who have lost their spouses, are guarding their finances, and are concerned about their health need different types of discussion than a couple of empty nesters in their fifties. Both are in the long process of living life, but both are in radically different stages of the process, so they need friends to whom they can relate and with whom they'll want to navigate the next few years. This is not to say that younger people shouldn't associate with older people. In fact, it's the experience and wisdom of our elders that can help us learn, grow, and avoid many heartaches in life. People need whomever they need. It is not the church's job to dictate who should connect with whom, but rather to help them find the people *they think* they need as they go through the various processes of life.

6. *Interaction*

Dr. Larry Crabb, in his book *Connecting*,[3] gives one of the strongest presentations I've ever read on the positive power of connecting with others. He says that relationships have a power for living that nothing else can provide. Certainly we all know that our lives with Christ provide power. But we tend to be less aware of the power that comes from the connectivity between people who are working through life together. Gayle and I have several friends who provide power for our lives that has gotten us through the most difficult stages of life. Without these friends, our lives wouldn't be anything like they are today.

I know many people who have tried to survive without the positive power of friendship, fellowship, and brother-/sisterhood, and all have failed miserably, or at least struggled unnecessarily. They were not connected. They didn't have power in their relationships. As I write this, I'm tempted to list some of our friendships in the body of Christ that have made our lives richer, but the list would be much too long and probably boring for you. Just sitting here thinking through them as I write makes me very grateful, because our lives have been filled with so many wonderful people.

I am so thankful for my friends. I love them, and sometimes it's hard for me to be productive because I always want to get together with them. They know my sins, and I know theirs. They coach me in managing and improving my weak areas and in capitalizing on my strong areas, and I do the same for them. They are my Camp David, where I can go to rest and refresh. We like to work, vacation, travel, get tired, relax, cook out, cry, laugh, get rich, go broke, and raise our kids together. We go to weddings and funerals together, spend sad nights and happy days together. We need to learn how to live life well so we can live a long life of friendship, love, and health together. Someday we'll begin to die, one at a time, and we need each other to do that well too.

Human beings are created to be relational in every stage of life. If we don't know how to do this well in the church, how can we ever hope to do it well in the rest of society? They know we are Christians because of our love for one another, right? But I daresay that most churches, most Christian ministries, and most discipleship systems are not known for overflowing love that is generated as people work through their programs. Some are, but most are not.

God is one, but He is also three persons existing in unique relationships with one another. The Father loves the Son and the Spirit, and they work together in harmony. The Son adores His Father and appreciates the work of the Spirit. The Spirit spends all of His time bringing glory to the Son and to the Father. They are three, in a positive, powerful, dynamic relationship with one another, so much so that they are one. Remember in Matthew 3:17 when the Father's voice parted the heavens and pealed out thunderous affirmation of Jesus' baptism? Most of us tend to envision an intimidating James Earl Jones voice admonishing onlookers. Not me. I imagine a proud Dad leaning over the balcony of heaven watching His Son whom He loves so much, angels trying to hold Him back from interrupting time, and He, so exuberant He can no longer contain Himself, parting the sky and hollering into the annals of human history, "That's My boy!"

This is the picture God has of us. He made us in His image and likeness, which means that we are intrinsically created to have positive, powerful relationships with others and that we are to become one with others. Thus, we can become one with Him through the blood of Christ and the work of the Holy Spirit. Christ is in us; we are in Him. We are one. In the same way, He expects us to become one with our spouses. And in some mystical way, the members of the body of Christ are to connect in fellowship with one another and in fellowship with Him so that we are one with each other—crying with the crying, rejoicing with the rejoicing, loving one another as we walk through life.

Too much is said about the systems of church, and not enough is said about the love of the church. No body of people on the earth knows love the way we do, but our systems shout so loud at times that by comparison, the whisper of our love is often inaudible. This is why I love free-market small groups: They thrive on love. People are not assigned to groups because of their neighborhoods, nor do they have to go anywhere or be nice to anyone because the church-government system orders them to do so. Instead, they follow the stream of His divine nature, and sometimes it leads to hiking beautiful mountains, going fishing, or sitting in a coffee shop talking about a good book. Other times it leads to hospital rooms, soup kitchens, and relief work in some war-torn area of the world. The river of God's love leads us to be with the people to whom we are drawn or whom we love the most, and our systems should facilitate it.

7. Multifaceted

Our churches aren't just victory churches for people in the best years of their lives. Nor are our churches filled with people who are just suffering through the most difficult years. Instead, our churches have people in every stage of life, experiencing every possible emotion. During any given service, there will be one person who has never been happier, sitting next to another who is falling through a deep tunnel of depression. If discipleship is not as multifaceted as the lives of the congregation, and if the church doesn't have a mechanism to change as rapidly as the lives of the people in the church, then the system that works well today might be obsolete and irrelevant next month.

How can our discipleship be flexible, relevant, and innovative? You know my answer. Use the power of freedom. Let people form their own small groups, and encourage them to enjoy the groups they are already in as long as they want to be in them. Let the one who is on top of the world create a group to share his secrets of success, and let the one who feels as if he is in the very depths of hell find a safe place to get the specific help he needs. Capitalize on the godly desires of the individuals to minister to others and the genuine needs of the individuals to be ministered to by others. Don't force ministry to happen in spite of the system; let the system facilitate ministry, in all of its many intriguing and wonderful facets. People reach people; systems serve people.

8. *Lifelong*

I've heard that the average family in America will move seven times in a lifetime. That's amazing to me. I can still return to Altamont, Kansas, to the home where my mother grew up during the Great Depression, and visit my cousin who lives on the same farmland that my family has been on for generations. I can spend time with friends who have known my family for many generations. I can go to Indiana to visit my sister, who lives in the same house that I grew up in thirty years ago. I can be pumping gas and have someone drive up that I haven't seen in years, and he will say, "Well, Teddy Haggard, how are you? Haven't seen you in a while." ("In a while" might mean fifteen to twenty years!)

In my mind, being the pastor of New Life Church in Colorado Springs for only seventeen years makes me a newcomer in the neighborhood. Unfortunately, that's not the norm anymore. More than 20 percent of the people in Colorado Springs move every year, which means many people in our church don't have roots. They are strangers, and they are vulnerable to the whims and breezes of life. It seems as though people change jobs, cities, spouses, and children the way they change clothes. As we know all too well, this type of living doesn't naturally produce connected people because it doesn't teach people to value longevity.

But we are the church. We need to do everything we can to connect people and help them develop stable, honorable lives—the kind of lives from which others draw joy and security. My desire is for a congregation full of people who can point to people they have been in relationship with for ten, twenty, or thirty years. My dad, who died years ago, had a friend named Pastor Jeff Floyd. Today, even though Mom and Dad have been in heaven for years, Pastor Jeff and his wife, Norma, visit my family in Colorado Springs from time to time. This is normal for us. Jeff and Norma have known me since I was in high school, and we will know and love one another for the rest of our lives. Pastor Jeff disciples me in life because he was a friend to my dad.

Our discipleship systems in our churches need to have lifelong longevity in mind. Last week my wife and I visited the Godly Homemakers small group in our church. It's been meeting for more than ten years. It used to be a private "ministry" of Thelma Miller, one of the ladies in our church, but when we started free-market small groups, it provided the structure Thelma needed to expand her ministry to more young women in the church. She's just doing what she was doing all along, but now she's doing it with the recognition and support she needed to be empowered for ministry.

Last Saturday, I performed a funeral for a family in our church. One of the ladies at the funeral told me that her prayer group has been meeting for seventeen years, since the first year of our church's existence. They were just a prayer group until we started free-market small groups, and now they have the structure and validity to keep going indefinitely.

At that funeral was a lady who led a small group that has evolved into a full-fledged ministry to women in the 10/40 Window. They pray specifically for the area on the globe that is considered least evangelized. This small group now has a multimillion-dollar budget with its own board and employees. But the core team still considers itself a small group under the authority of our church. They will minister to those in need in the 10/40 Window for the rest of their lives.

See, this isn't just a program. It's a community of empowerment filled with love and compassion. It's a lifelong commitment to disciple others with His purpose in mind. It's not a program to try or a quick fix to employ; it's a lifestyle to embrace. It's a concept of the family of God working in groups according to the leading of the Lord. It's power for a lifetime, which explains why our back-door rate went from 20 percent a year to less than five percent when we started free-market small groups.

9. Christlikeness

Finally, the most important ingredient of successful discipleship is Christlikeness. Jesus commanded the church to *make disciples*. Disciples of whom? John the Baptist had disciples. Aristotle and Plato had disciples. In the business world, both Jack Welch and Bill Gates have disciples. At the end of His life, Jesus looked in the eyes of His own disciples—His followers, imitators, and workers—and instructed them to make from all nations disciples of Himself, like themselves. "Be fruitful and multiply," He told them, in essence. And so even now, two millennia later, the core of discipleship is making people more like Jesus.

The tendency among many discipleship ministries, departments, and programs is to bring the discipleship candidates to themselves. Standardize them, homogenize them, and package them to sell. The only problem is, we are making people, not eggnog. Consumers expect to buy a quart of eggnog during the holiday season and have it taste like all the other eggnog they've had in their lives. They expect it, consciously or unconsciously, to be clean and free of pathogens. And thankfully, here in America, anyway, that's how they get it. On the other hand, *people* are, if they are any one thing, *different*. What works for one fails for another. What appeals to one bores another. It's the same old problem Communist countries like the former Soviet Union kept running into. People are different, and if we are effectively going to make disciples of them, we have to go where they are.

Remember the way Jesus discipled? He rarely called all the people to Him and told them what to do. (Actually, when He did instruct the masses, it was because they had *followed* Him.) No, Jesus went to the people. He spent the vast majority of His three-year ministry career traveling around, seeing people, and serving them. Finding them where they were, for better and for worse, and loving them. To be Christlike means, among other things, to serve people wherever they are—to go where they are and bring Christ to them.

When we talk about golfing, sewing, fishing, hiking, and mentoring, sometimes people wonder if these are really the most effective ways to disciple others. But I have no doubt about it. I also have little doubt that people wondered whether Jesus' touching lepers, dining with tax collectors, and fishing with the sons of Zebedee were the most effective ways to disciple others. We all face the challenge of integrating biblical principles into every portion of our lives, and free-market small groups help make it so that every portion of our lives—even our hobbies—have spiritual significance.

Discipleship is not a linear process that says learn A, then go to B, then try C, and then you are ready for D. If human beings were like this, Communism would have worked. But humans don't work that way. They may start on A, but then their dad comes home drunk and they have an

H issue that causes them to have an L discussion with the understanding of an A.

What does this mean? It means we have to disciple people in the midst of their walks, in the center of their interests, moving them in the direction of God's perfect plan for their lives. Our lives are not linear. We don't go from one point to the next in a straight line. Our lives are like rivers. They flow according to a series of points of least resistance. That's why we swerve back and forth, to and fro. But with a healthy church that adapts to us as we grow, we can reach Z with great satisfaction and joy in our lives.

CHAPTER TEN

Embracing Individuality

I'm writing from a little town in the mountains of Colorado. As I look out the window, I can see at least twenty small businesses. Each business expresses the particular personality and preferences of its owner. Each provides something different in a unique style. Some of the businesses appear similar to others from the outside, but if I were to go inside I'd find a unique array of products, services, and selling techniques. Thankfully, the government didn't tell any of these owners what they had to sell. The government did make sure that they all have safe structural, electrical, and septic systems in their buildings, and the government will keep them from doing any illegal activity (theoretically), but the nature of the business is the choice of the business owners. If the public finds their products or services useful, the businesses will prosper. If not, the owners will have to come up with something better or join up with an organization whose output the public prefers.

Look through the Yellow Pages or glance down the business district of any town, and you'll see a wide variety of business ideas that reflect a vast array of individual tastes and needs. Lots of different types of businesses can flourish because there are so many different types of people, and as long as the government gives people freedom to develop ideas, the nature of business can be infinitely diverse. There are hundreds of businesses that you'll never use, but that doesn't mean they are irrelevant to everyone. Someone will use them, or else they'll die out and be replaced by better businesses. I've never needed a taxidermist, but there's a thriving taxidermy business in southern Colorado Springs. I like the new theaters with great big seats, loud speakers, and huge screens, so I'd probably never go to the art house movie theater downtown, but there is a market for art movies in Colorado Springs, and the little downtown theater caters to that market. The businesses in my town don't reflect just *my* tastes—they reflect the wide range of tastes and needs in my town.

Now think of your own church or ministry. Every Christian you know has a desire to serve people, and that desire will only be satisfied when discipling others in an effective, life-giving way. You can either encourage and capitalize on that desire by letting it flourish within appropriate guidelines, or you can thwart it by forcing it into compliance with an unnecessarily strict system. People are so varied that it's impossible to imagine all of them teaching the same thing, the same way, on the same night, to the same size groups. That may sound great to the theoretician, but it's just not practical.

Instead, it's much more natural and powerful to design a basic set of standards and requirements that can apply to the variety—just as the same water, septic, and power regulations apply to all businesses whether they fix people's hair or repair their teeth—and then allow individual personality types, gift mixes, experiences, interests, and stages of life to determine what ministries will actually look like.

To the more rigid systems, the diversity of age, experience, personality, gifts, and interests of the congregation is a problem to be dealt with, an obstacle to be hurdled. If only people were all the same! Then what a utopia our same-number, same-night, same-subject cell groups would be! But as we have already discussed, people are different. And if we are willing to concede this truth—the way aircraft designers have conceded the truth of gravity—it can switch from being the one pesky factor that keeps our small-group ministry from working to being the bedrock strength of our discipleship.

In the free-market system, the diversity of age, experience, personality, gifts, and interests is a strength rather than a point of conflict. The more people who join the system, the more people who can be reached by the system. The free market is inclusive, not exclusive. It guarantees that people's individual gifts will be used to their maximum potentials. The free-market system helps people do whatever they naturally do best, rather than forcing them to do something awkward and unfamiliar. It simply capitalizes on their natural strengths.

MANY GIFTS, MANY EXPRESSIONS

The Christian church has always flourished under the influence of new personalities and gifts. Think of the three Great Awakenings in recent American history. Jonathan Edwards in the eighteenth century preached the gospel in strict fire-and-brimstone terms, and the Spirit of God was evident in his revival meetings as people threw themselves at the altar. In the early nineteenth century, Charles Finney focused more on man's need to repent than on God's wrath, and his words motivated people to surrender themselves to God. D. L. Moody traveled all over the country in the late nineteenth century, preaching that the sinner was a drowning victim and that Jesus was coming in His lifeboat to save him, and his timely techniques resonated with the audience of his time. Historians like to weigh the revivalists against one another, but I believe God used them all in ways that were appropriate to their times. Each spoke based on his own personality and gifts. In the annals of Christian history, ministers like these and others aren't at war with one another, but are working together in various ways to expand the kingdom of God.

The contemporary church works the same way. Different Christians have different approaches to ministry that are based on their individual mixes of personality types, interests, and spiritual gifts. We've talked a lot about personality and interests, so I want to devote some time here to discussing the differences between individual mixes of spiritual gifts. In this chapter, I want to give you a simple, biblical understanding of the variety of ways people can express themselves individually in the body of Christ through the unique mix of gifts God has given them (By the way, if you want a great book on spiritual gifts, I recommend *Discovering Your Spiritual Gifts*, by Dr. C. Peter Wagner. [Regal, 2002].)

The idea that people are different isn't a modern notion. The apostle Paul understood it very well, and he talked about it clearly in terms of the diverse gifts God has given believers and the way the Spirit manifests Himself differently in all of us. Understanding these individual mixes of gifts and the ways they are expressed will help us employ them in our churches and ministries to their fullest extent. The main idea here comes from 1 Corinthians 12:4–7, which says, "There are different kinds of *gifts*, but the same Spirit. There are different kinds of *service*, but the same Lord. There are different kinds of working, but the same God works all of them in all men. Now to each one the *manifestation* of the Spirit is given for the common good" (emphasis mine). In other words, God works through each of us in wildly different ways according to our dominant gifts, the ways we like to serve, and how we manifest the Spirit of God. It's vital for us to recognize and appreciate those differences in the body of Christ.

Motivational Gifts

Everyone has a "motivational gift." In other words, while God gives all of us a variety of gifts, we all have a gift that motivates us more than any other. Let's look at the seven gifts listed in Romans 12:6–8 and see how each one can be dominant in a person's life:

> We have different gifts, according to the grace given us. If a man's gift is *prophesying*, let him use it in proportion to his faith. If it is *serving*, let him serve; if it is *teaching*, let him teach; if it is *encouraging*, let him encourage; if it is *contributing* to the needs of others, let him give generously; if it is *leadership*, let him govern diligently; if it is *showing mercy*, let him do it cheerfully. (italics mine)

Prophesying: Saying What God Says. All of the Scriptures are prophetic, which is to say that they are the very words of God. When a person's primary motivational gift is prophecy, he or she is a strong adherent to the particulars of God's heart, thoughts, and actions. Some of the time, people with the gift of prophecy can be difficult for others to deal with. They often seem opinionated and passionate. They love to proclaim truth loudly, and they love to condemn sinfulness just as loudly. Remember Samuel's confrontation of Saul, Nathan's rebuke of David, and John the Baptist's condemnation of Herod and his wife? These men did not seem particularly concerned with pandering to the one in power, padding their judgment of his sin, or preserving their own emotional well-being. These were not *sensitive* men. The prophetically gifted are direct in their speech because they desperately want others to know the will of God. Though it can be hard to handle people with this gift, I'm always a strong defender of prophecy when it's used wisely. We all need to understand the voice of God, and it's worth working with people with this gift.

Serving: Taking Care of the Needs of Others. Mother Teresa said, "Faith in action is love. Love in action is service."[1] Just as all Christians should say what God says, all Christians should be servants. However, those with a dominant motivational gift of serving are more prone to look for opportunities to take care of others and love doing it. These people are happiest expressing love by what they do. They prefer taking care of the needs of others rather than their own needs. They are filled with kindness, compassion, and hearts to reach out to others.

Servants make every ministry work well. They are easily taken advantage of, and they don't seem to mind, so it's important to protect them. They are willing to go out at night for another, repair a stranger's car, or care for children in a difficult situation. I love these people, and I think they're the backbone of any strong ministry.

Three years ago, we had a blizzard unusually early in the season for Colorado. Over the course of two late-October days, more than three feet of snow fell on our city. Of course, few people had yet put on their snow tires, packed the tire chains in the trunk, and made all the other usual preparations for winter driving here, because nobody was expecting snow. So imagine the scene: roads snow- and ice-packed, visibility virtually zero, cars spun off to the side of the street, cars in the medians, cars facing the wrong way, cars in drainage ditches—cars just about everywhere they are not supposed to be.

That night Eli Winningham, a young man in our church with a very large truck, drove around town towing cars out of ditches, pushing them back on the road, pulling them out of snowdrifts, and jump-starting them when they were stalled. Eli never slept that night. He just kept serving and serving and serving.

Nobody called Eli and told him to help these people. Nobody expected it of him, and nobody would have been disappointed with him if he had stayed home that night. Probably nobody would have even thought about it. But he is gifted by God to serve, and it's what he loves to do. He asks no compensation and seeks no recognition. He just serves because God has called him to serve, and he is a tremendous blessing to our church and our city.

Teaching: Informing Others of Something They Didn't Know Before. People motivated by teaching love researching a subject and communicating it so it can be understood. They also love outlines and they love seeing people take notes. Teachers thrive on the discovery and dissemination of truth. Learning makes them happy. To use our DISC terms, an I teacher is very different from a C teacher. C teachers are happy when every detail is correct, and less concerned about how it makes the student feel. An I teacher may want the details right, but is more concerned about the feelings of the students.

Josh McDowell is the consummate teacher. He has taken a subject he is passionate about—defending the historicity of Jesus' life, death, and resurrection—and studied, traveled, and researched until he has become an expert. Always motivated by the desire for people to grasp the truth, he has made a career of communicating his findings. He has shared his message in more than sixty countries and on more than eight hundred university and high-school campuses. He has written some of the most comprehensive and persuasive material available on the subject, including *More Than a Carpenter*, *He Walked Among Us* (coauthored with Bill Wilson), *Evidence That Demands a Verdict, Volumes I and II*, and *A Ready Defense*, just to name a few. And now in virtually all Christian circles, his name is synonymous with *evidence*. Josh McDowell's gift of teaching has led to thousands trusting Christ and has made him one of the primary defenders of the Christian faith.

Encouraging: Delivering Hope. When I preach a sermon that isn't very good, I really don't want to hear from those who are motivated by prophecy or teaching. I'm sure I'll hear from them later in the week, but right after a mediocre sermon, I need an encourager to come up and talk to me. It's not that encouragers flatter; it's that in the midst of darkness, they can find a ray of light. In the midst of a storm, they can create an island of tranquillity. They are a strength to any ministry—they help keep it positive and moving forward. Nearly everyone knows how to be an encourager, but people who have the dominant motivational gift of encouragement are always on the lookout for someone who needs a comforting word.

Fitzgerald's Gatsby is the classic encourager. Everybody's friend, the lovable eccentric just had a way of being exactly what people needed at *that* moment:

> He smiled understandingly—much more than understandingly. It was one of those rare smiles with a quality of eternal reassurance in it, that you may come across four or five times in life. It faced . . . the whole external world for an instant, and then concentrated on you with an irresistible prejudice in your favor. It understood you just as far as you wanted to be understood, believed in you as you would like to believe in yourself, and assured you that it had precisely the impression of you that, at your best, you hoped to convey.[2]

Those motivated by the gift of encouragement are our shelters, our safe havens. They stand up for us even when we are wrong, speak softly to us even when we are blunt, and believe in us when we have trouble believing in ourselves. Their role in the Body is as unique and unmistakable as it is critical.

Giving: Enjoying Using Your Resources for Great Purposes. Givers are the people who enjoy investing in projects, supporting missions, equipping churches, and endowing philanthropic causes. They give their time, resources, and finances, sometimes out of their own need. They actually enjoy offerings. They don't mind pastors, Christian broadcasters, and others taking time to explain why financial investment in their projects is valuable.

There are several people at New Life who have a primary motivational gift of giving. They all think I should talk more about money and have more fund-raisers. They love big projects. They love to see their investment producing results for others. Because they thrive on giving, they enjoy reading financial reports from benevolent organizations and are interested in the subtleties of these reports—not because they are critical, but because they are givers and they enjoy knowing that their investments make a difference in the lives of people.

Leadership: Motivating Others. Those whose motivational gift is leadership have vision. They will, if needed, take charge and motivate people to make vision reality. Most megachurch pastors have leadership as one of their motivational gifts. They are task-oriented and like to make sure people are working together toward a goal. The best leaders know when to take charge, when to submit to the leadership of another, and when to establish or cooperate with a system so people can *produce*. When a leader is wise and does the right thing, incredible anointing flows.

Thomas Jefferson, our third president and the primary author of the Constitution, was a powerful and effective leader. Detailed, ordered, and driven, he had a vision of where America was headed and had a passion for bringing Americans on board with that vision. "In an age of imperialism," writes Stephen Ambrose, "he was the greatest empire builder of all. His mind encompassed the continent." Jefferson believed that the destiny of America was to stretch from sea to shining sea as one nation, and he acted on that belief systematically throughout his time in office. Driven by the idea of an "Empire of Liberty," he was at the same time "keenly sensitive to the needs and dreams of his constituents." He loved the people he was serving. The essence of Thomas Jefferson's presidency was the wise and practical integration of these two values, and the results of it are vast. We owe much of what our nation is today to his leadership.[3]

Mercy: Caring. People who are motivated by mercy cry during sad scenes in movies, stop to care for others in the mall or on the street, and are very concerned for the less fortunate. They do things for the underprivileged. They reach out, and if they have a secondary gift of leadership, they motivate people to reach out and care for others as well. Mercy-motivated people will often help care for others to the point at which they place themselves in jeopardy. Mercy-motivated people are great doctors and nurses (especially if they are C's). They are wonderful in dealing with children, the wounded, and the handicapped.

My father was motivated by mercy, and I remember his stopping in the middle of a busy schedule to take care of a poor person or to help someone in need. He spent money he didn't have to help others. He would regularly pay the grocery bill for someone he would see in the store who was obviously poor or in financial trouble.

Again, everyone around us has one or two of these gifts as their primary motivation. Senior pastors and ministry leaders need to use a system that capitalizes on all the gifts by empowering everyone within their reach. If we are in a community of believers that is pastored by a person who projects his own motivational gift onto the entire church, then the ministry will be narrow in its scope. But if that leader empowers everyone in their own individual gifts, then the ministry's reach is limitless. In fact, it doesn't matter what motivational gift the pastor or those in leadership have if they understand that their role is to provide a system so that anyone, with any gift mix, can have a valid role in the community in discipling others.

Services

Remember that Paul says "there are different kinds of service" too. First Corinthians 12:27–31 gives us an indication of various ways people serve:

> Now you are the body of Christ, and each one of you is a part of it. And in the church God has appointed first of all *apostles*, second *prophets*, third *teachers*, then *workers of miracles*, also those having gifts of *healing*, those able to *help others*, those with gifts of *administration*, and those *speaking in different kinds of tongues*. Are all apostles? Are all prophets? Are all teachers? Do all work miracles? Do all have gifts of healing? Do all speak in tongues? Do all interpret? But eagerly desire the greater gifts. (italics mine)

Now, some of these terms and definitions sound similar to those we've already discussed. But before we were talking about what motivates us, and now we are talking about different ways of serving. And portions of the Scripture above relate to material we'll be discussing in the section that follows such as speaking in tongues and interpreting tongues. These are not cold, clean categories that we can fit people into squarely. Rather, this is a way of describing the various mixes of gifts, service ministries, and manifestations of God's Spirit that exist in any Christian community.

Apostles. An apostle is one who is sent out. These are missionaries who build up works where there were none before. Church planters do apostolic ministry as well as those in our churches who build works in unreached places. The services of apostles are needed in dark jungles, Laundromats, and board rooms. Apostolic service always reaches out into the darkness.

Prophets. Prophetic ministry proclaims the truth with assurance. This ministry says it straight and with accuracy.

Teachers. Teaching ministry is information based. It communicates truth with the goal of increasing the understanding of the hearers.

Workers of Miracles. The ministry of the miraculous is the ministry of answered prayer. It demonstrates the validity of the risen Christ. It proves that Christianity isn't just a belief system or a dead religion, but is a powerful life.

Healing. Healing ministry is one of words and action. It's when the power of God touches people and restores them in their bodies, souls, and/or minds.

Helps. The ministry of helps is very practical. It moves furniture, fixes situations, and lends a hand. It's practical service.

Administration. The ministry of administration establishes systems so life works better for everyone. Administration ensures that the oil gets changed on time, that tires are rotated, and that the carpets are cleaned on a schedule.

The circle of believers that you are responsible to disciple is made up of a variety of people. They have differing personality types, various motivational gifts, and they express their service to God in a variety of ways. But that's not all. In addition to this, those who are filled with the Holy Spirit have the manifestations of the Holy Spirit working in them.

Manifestations

The manifestations of the Holy Spirit are listed in 1 Corinthians 12:7–11, where Paul wrote:

> Now to each one the manifestation of the Spirit is given for the common good. To one there is given through the Spirit the *message of wisdom*, to another the *message of knowledge* by means of the same Spirit, to another *faith* by the same Spirit, to another *gifts of healing* by that one Spirit, to another *miraculous powers*, to another *prophecy*, to another *distinguishing between spirits*, to another *speaking in different kinds of tongues*, and to still another the *interpretation of tongues*. All these are the work of one and the same Spirit, and he gives them to each one, just as he determines. (italics mine)

Wisdom: Wisdom is knowing what to do with what we know. It includes the power to manage our hearts, thoughts, speech, and actions.

Knowledge: Knowledge involves perceiving thoughts, concepts, and ideas. This is data, facts, information. Knowledge is understanding, thinking, and working with big ideas, philosophies, and theologies.

Faith: Simply put, faith is confidence in God.

Healing: This is God's power working through our speech and actions to heal people.

Miracles: In miracles, God's power overrides natural law. Again, miracles prove the supremacy of the kingdom of God in a given situation.

Prophecy: Prophets speak God's thoughts into a situation.

Discernment: A person with this gift knows the difference between the work of the human spirit, angels, demonic spirits, and the Holy Spirit. This is recognizing the subtle differences between the voice of God, the voice of darkness, and the voice of self, or catching the difference between the truth and a lie.

Tongues: This is the Holy Spirit's language of prayer speaking through us directly to God the Father.

Interpretation: Interpreters express in their own language what the Holy Spirit has been praying.

OK, OK, enough. People are different from one another, and they express themselves in the body of Christ in different ways. Why is this so important? Because if it is true, imagine what a mistake we've made trying to get all of them to study the same thing at the same time. The style of ministry in most churches reflects the senior pastor, the denominational curriculum, or the culture of the church, not the congregation. So, those who can join with the dominant trend in the church do. But those who can't, either conform, become tolerant, or leave.

But the church is not about one exclusive stream. It's about equipping and building up the *people* in the church. The congregation is not there to fulfill the senior pastor's vision. They aren't there to serve his ministry. He is there to serve *their* ministries. Senior pastors have been given authority to serve their congregations.

Let me try to say this a different way: The church is not about the institution. It's about the people. The church does not prop up the ministry or the pastor. The pastor builds up the people to minister. He is there to equip them for *their* ministries. Why would we want to homogenize people into the same mold? God made every person unique, and the diversity of God's creation in individuals is a strength to His kingdom, not a weakness. This is why I love free-market small groups. This system recognizes that everyone is a minister and that everything can be a ministry. Dog training, fly-fishing, algebra, the book of Romans, marriage class, financial planning, serving at the soup kitchen, writing a check, and on and on. All are ministry. All are discipleship. All are important.

CHAPTER ELEVEN

Love and Friendship: The Wellspring of Good Ministry

MARK TWAIN TELLS THE TIMELESS STORY OF THE FRIENDSHIP between Tom Sawyer and Huck Finn. Sneaking out in the middle of the night, digging for buried treasure, pretending to be pirates, swimming in the muddy banks of the Mississippi River, the two are the best of friends. There's something about these boys that is captivating. Mischievous as they are, they seem to bring out the best in each other. Imagination, resourcefulness, compassion, loyalty—what major life lessons did Tom and Huck not learn growing up together on the bayou? And how much they enjoyed each other! Who doesn't want a friend like Huck? I smile when I remember the two boys' oath of allegiance to one another:

"Now, look-a-here, Tom, let's take and swear to one another . . ."

"I'm agreed . . . would you just hold hands and swear that we—"

"Oh, no, that wouldn't do for this. That's good enough for little rubbishy common things—specially with gals, cuz *they* go back on you anyway, and blab if they get in a huff—but there orter be writing 'bout a big thing like this. And blood."

Tom's whole being applauded this idea. It was deep, and dark, and awful; the hour, the circumstances, the surroundings, were in keeping with it.[1]

Please understand that I am not endorsing "blood brother" covenants. However, I do believe that strong, committed, faithful friendships are the building blocks of successful living. Throughout the Bible, love and friendship are described as values that empower people in God's plan for their lives. From Joshua to David, from Jesus to Paul, close relationships are keys to success. Why is it, then, that in the contemporary evangelical church we act as if organizational structures and programs baptized in Bible teaching are the secrets to successful ministry? Many ministries have a reputation for having efficient systems, but too often that efficiency comes at the expense of people. Unfortunately, some ministries are not known for the longevity of their employees—they hire people, burn them out, throw them away, and start again with new people.

Love should be the cornerstone of everything we do in Jesus' name. The fruit of every local church should be wholesome families and long-lasting, healthy friendships. There is a reason why the Scriptures highlight not just individual people, but *friendships*: Moses and Aaron, David and Jonathan, Mary and Elizabeth, Jesus and John, Paul and Timothy. Certainly, we all value corporate ministry systems and their ability to maintain order and stimulate activity. Every type of organization has to have such systems in place. But we Christians also believe that strong relationships and love should play a key role in any ministry. God wants His followers to be known because of their love for one another, and it's often hard to show love when working strictly according to the organizational flowchart. I believe that free-market ministry gives us both the order necessary for organizing a group of people, and the system that accommodates and accomplishes God's love through people rather than thwarting it.

First John 4:16 says God is love. But I can only think of one major church conference I've ever attended that offered workshops on the subject of love.

Most conferences don't even mention it, except maybe in worship songs. We talk about style, marketing, city-reaching strategies, and being seeker friendly. But Jesus didn't say, "They will know you by your style of music." He said, "By this all men will know that you are my disciples, if you love one another" (John 13:35). So why aren't we talking about love? Maybe it feels too goofy and mushy. Or maybe it's too subjective. No doubt, it has been abused. My fear, though, is that we don't talk much about it because we don't know very much about it. It's much easier to sound confident talking about evangelism statistics and Gen-X, postmodern service styles.

I'm convinced that we're living in a love-starved world, which means that it's time for all of us to get over our hesitations talking about love, start learning love, and adjust our systems to actually encourage love. If God is love, there's nothing to be embarrassed about. We've spent ten chapters together emphasizing the importance of respecting individuals, understanding the way people naturally group, and facilitating people in their ministries. Now I want to talk with you about the glue that holds everything together. I want to talk with you about love and friendship and how they are the wellspring of all good ministry.

Don't skip this chapter. Instead, slow down and read it carefully. Think about it. As I mentioned earlier, all human beings are made in the image and likeness of God. Because God is Father, Son, and Holy Spirit in perfect relationship with one another, all human beings desire to be in relationships. Human beings strive for connectivity with God and with one another, and that connectivity is one of the keys to successful ministry.

No, I'm wrong about that. I didn't say that right. Let me try again. Love is *the* one and only key to genuine ministry. There, that's better. If a church or ministry is serious about connecting people together, we have to know what love and friendship are all about, and we have to be able to live in love and friendship with one another. I know this may sound simplistic. That is not my intent. But I do want to draw a distinction between God-oriented corporate ministry that offers a well-packaged God (and of course, plenty of God products) and God's own supernatural river of the flow of His love that can be intentionally integrated into the life of the church.

THE GRAND EXPERIMENT

I've often said that our church is an experiment in love. For years people have told me that pastors shouldn't be allowed to hire their friends and that they shouldn't encourage the people on staff to be close friends with one another. And for years I've ignored that advice. My staff is populated with some of Gayle's and my very best friends, and many more of our best friends attend the church. We are friends, and we all work well together. We still butt heads from time to time, but at the end of the day, we are all faithful, honorable friends. We don't use our friendships as leverage against one another, and we don't slack off in our productivity, either. We have all the dynamics of a strong local church structure, plus friendship.

My biggest problem as pastor of New Life is that I enjoy the people working here so much that I can't stay away. Gayle and I have hired the people we love. When I'm at the office, I want to hang out in the youth department, go to lunch with the crew from the children's department, or go over to the World Prayer Center and talk about the power of God with the team. Often, just standing around in the hallway and brainstorming new ideas is a great way to invest time. We want our offices next to one another's so we can connect. We love MBWA (Management By Wandering Around) because we enjoy one another and the work that we do together so much. The atmosphere of our church is dynamic and lively because of the rich love we all have for one another.

I'm writing this chapter in Niwot, Colorado. When I finish, I will forward it to Patton Dodd, a friend of mine in Boston. Patton will be the first to read through this chapter. He'll ensure that it clearly communicates the ideas that we practice here at New Life. Patton and I have worked well together for several years not just because we have a professional working relationship, but because we love each other. We desire God's best for each other. We enjoy each other's company. We pray for each other. That's valuable, and fortunately, it makes us work together better than it would if Patton were just some faceless guy who could edit.

After he sends this back to me, I'll write it again and then forward it to Rob Brendle, who will read it through and check to make sure the Scripture and book references are correct. Today, Rob and his wife left on a week-long vacation to the Caribbean. Last night he called me, wanting some of the chapters of this book to read on his vacation. At first, I refused to send them. I told him that I didn't want him working for me or thinking about my ideas while on vacation. But Rob said that he wanted to because he loved me and wanted to ensure that we would have this material to the publisher on time. He didn't feel obligated because of corporate pressure to get the job done. He felt the compulsion of love. (I didn't let him take any chapters to edit, and we didn't have it to the publisher on time.)

Then it goes to Ted Whaley, the Director of Small-Group Ministry at our church. Ted and I met as freshmen in college, were roommates together, and traveled in ministry together. I performed his wedding to Denise, and he played the piano at my mother's funeral. We serve together because of calling and friendship. Ted knows how people connect, so when he's done with the manuscript, Gayle and I will read it and make all the final adjustments before I send it to Thomas Nelson, Inc. (Of course, by the time you read this, all of this will have taken place, but at the time of this writing, this is all still in the future.)

Why Thomas Nelson? Because a man named Victor Oliver, who ministers to others through his work at Thomas Nelson, heard me speak on several occasions. He believes in my message and knows that if there isn't a reformation in the way we mobilize people within our churches, the body of Christ might not be as productive as it could have been otherwise. There are lots of publishers who do great work, but Victor believes strongly in this particular message. He loves these ideas, and he loves me.

Now, let me make a couple of clarifying remarks here. I believe in the importance of love and connectivity. But I also believe that when a church hires someone, it is hiring that person to do exceptional work. Patton, Rob, Ted, and I share the love of Christ. But Patton, Rob, and Ted are not slouches, and I couldn't use their help if they were. They are not lazy; they don't do sloppy work; they are not thoughtless. They perform well. I sense God's love in Victor Oliver at Thomas Nelson, but Thomas Nelson Publishers is also a first-class Christian publisher. If it wasn't, Victor and I would know one another as men serving Christ together, but Victor wouldn't be able to offer me the quality services of Thomas Nelson, which would hurt the communication of this *incredible* book!

Sorry, I lost myself for a moment.

So, when we hire a church staff, we need a divine flow with the people who work with us closely, and we also need for them to be strong workers. And of course, we don't hire everyone we love. I have a divine flow with lots of people we don't hire in the church either because we don't need their particular expertise or because they need to increase their skill levels. And we have hired many people whom I didn't know at first. But I want us all to be friends, and everyone who works at New Life knows it's a loving, friendly environment.

Over and over again, I've had people tell me that it's too loose, that I need to have more control, that if I let my staff be too friendly, they'll walk all over me and one another. They may be right, but it hasn't happened yet. We're seventeen years into this experiment called New Life Church, and so far, so good. I don't worry at all about what the dissenters say. Why? Because I trust these people. They're my friends, and even if it doesn't make sense to some of the church-growth theorists or organizational specialists, it makes sense to us.

New Life Church is a grand experiment in love, and when we love, the experiment always works. We have efficient systems in place, but when it comes down to choosing to honor the system or people, we honor people. If the red tape needs to be cut in order to help someone, we don't hesitate to pull out the scissors. Our team is a family of love that works well together to make it hard for people to go to hell from Colorado Springs.

DEFINING LOVE

Several years ago I came across a definition of love in a book called *Who Cares About Love* by Win Arn, Carroll Nyquist, and Charles Arn:

> Love is intentionally doing something caring or helpful for another person, in Jesus' name, regardless of the cost or consequence to oneself.[2]

There are several elements in this definition that I like.

Intentionality:

This means that true love is different from the often temporary emotions that accompany falling in love. This love certainly has an element of emotion, but it's primarily a decision. To love others genuinely means to show them love *on purpose*. The direction of our hearts is up to us, and when we choose to love God, we also choose to become a conduit of His love to other people. We choose to become His hand in someone else's life. We choose to be the answer to one's prayers, or to provide the solution to a need in another's life. Sometimes those needs are physical, sometimes mental, and other times emotional. It doesn't matter, because when we are intentional about demonstrating love, we can find a way to meet the needs of others. The only limitation occurs if a person rejects what we would like to do. If one does, that's fine. God faces the same problem every day. But most people are open to some expression of love.

Doing Something:

Love is not just a feeling or an emotion. Love is something that can be seen. Others can observe it. Love is empirical. Sending a card, giving a gift, offering a loving touch, speaking a kind word, investing time with a person, doing something to serve others—these are tangible expressions of love. When we say we love someone but don't do anything to demonstrate love, we lie. First John 3:18 exhorts, "Let us not love with words or tongue but with actions and in truth." True love always manifests itself. When you have love for someone, that love should be observable by you, him, and an outsider who is watching.

Caring:

Caring for someone means that you've been moved by his situation, emotions, or circumstances. Caring means that you are doing something in particular that will make that person feel better about life, or cause that individual's situation to improve because you have concern for him. It is an assignment of value. It is a function of the heart.

Helpful:

Here again is a reminder that an act of love is a practical, physical thing you can do to solve an actual problem someone is facing: moving furniture, cleaning the person's house, cooking a meal for that family, repairing a furnace, mowing his grass, or maintaining his car. A popular song by Michael W. Smith contends, "Love isn't really love / Till you give it away."

For Another Person:

It's impossible to love in a vacuum. You've heard it said that love is a verb. Well, there are certain verbs in the English language that require an indirect object. "To hit" necessitates a thing or person that is being hit. "To believe" requires an idea *being* adhered to. *Love* is one of these verbs. Love always reaches outside of ourselves toward another person.

We are commanded to love God and love our neighbors because it forces us to look externally. Selfish and self-centered people have difficulty loving either God or their neighbors. Love should always flow out of us because of God's love flowing into us.

In Jesus' Name:

It's impossible to love wisely and powerfully unless we're filled with the love of God. No other people of faith build schools, hospitals, orphanages, and other service institutions the way Christians do. We enjoy loving others because of Jesus' love for us. We don't force the people we help to believe and worship the way we do, even though we welcome that. We take care of others simply to demonstrate the love of Christ, regardless of their responses. We do it as His representatives and because He loved us first.

Regardless of the Cost or Consequence to Oneself:

In economics, we teach the concept of *opportunity cost*. There is a price associated with every endeavor, whether it be money or time or attention, which could otherwise be spent on something else. Everything is a trade-off. If our government wants to spend more money on public education, it will have to decide to spend less money on transportation or farm subsidy or defense. Demonstrating love costs us something. It may cost us time, or money, or energy, or the ability to do something for ourselves.

My parents demonstrated their love for me by financing my way through school, helping me buy a car, and many other tangible sacrifices they made to communicate their love for me. Jesus demonstrated His love for us at the cost of His life. The miracle of love is that it costs something wonderful, but then is multiplied to make the world a better place, one person at a time.

LET LOVE RULE

God loves people, and He wants to demonstrate His love for people through us. We are His vessels. We are His ambassadors. We are His cola-borers. We are His hands extended. We are the demonstration of His heart on the earth. We are to be instruments of His love.

Second John 6 says, "And this is love: that we walk in obedience to his commands. As you have heard from the beginning, his command is that you walk in love." To walk in love is to be guided by it and follow its lead, to let love determine the relationships we have, the places we go, the thoughts we think, and the things we do. This is what Jesus did when He ministered to the crowds. He let His heart guide His actions. The Bible says in Matthew 9:36, "When he saw the crowds, he had compassion on them, because they were harassed and helpless, like sheep without a shepherd." Likewise, Matthew 14:14 says, "When Jesus landed and saw a large crowd, he had compassion on them and healed their sick."

What moved Jesus? It was divine compassion rising up in His heart. You can be sure that there were times when Jesus would have much preferred to pray, be alone with His disciples, or just sleep! But He felt what the late John Osteen, a great preacher in Houston, Texas, used to call the "divine flow of God's love." God's love flowed toward the multitudes, and Jesus followed that flow so that the healing love of God could relieve people's suffering. In my twenty-five years of ministry experience, the greatest lesson I've learned is to follow the divine flow of God's love, letting it direct me and connect me to others.

Many people look at Jesus' example and get stuck. We just don't *feel* love for this person or that person. Lest we get hung up on the feelings, let me caution you that love has little to do with how you feel about someone. C. S. Lewis explained this profoundly: "Do not waste time bothering whether you 'love' your neighbor; act as if you did. As soon as we do this we find one of the great secrets. When you are behaving as if you loved someone, you will presently come to love him."[3] In acting as if we love others— inasmuch as the acts are intentional, helpful, reflect care for them, and cost us something—we *are* loving them.

Don't get me wrong. I'm not advocating being fake, doing nice things but inwardly harboring resentment and bitterness; rather I'm suggesting just taking our eyes off ourselves and how we feel and fixing them on other people. This is love.

I mentioned 1 John 4 earlier, but let's look at some verses in that chapter closely. I know you've read these before on your own, but read them again. Read them over and over again until you get it, because God is using John to communicate to us powerful, life-shaping ideas about love:

Dear friends, let us love one another, for love comes from God. Everyone who loves has been born of God and knows God. Whoever does not love does not know God, because God is love . . . Whoever lives in love lives in God, and God in him. In this way, love is made complete among us so that we will have confidence on the day of judgment, because in this world we are like him. There is no fear in love. But perfect love drives out fear, because fear has to do with punishment. The one who fears is not made perfect in love. We love because he first loved us. If anyone says, "I love God," yet hates his brother, he is a liar. For anyone who does not love his brother, whom he has seen, cannot love God, whom he has not seen. And he has given us this command: Whoever loves God must also love his brother. (1 John 4:7–8; 16–21)

Of course, we can't operate in the divine flow if there is sin in our hearts. Love can be confusing because some mix it with sexuality, inordinate spiritual connections, and superficial manipulation. But when I talk about the divine flow, I'm talking about the perfect and pure love of God in our hearts flowing through us toward another person. I'm not talking about sexual attraction, strange spiritual connectivity, or a tool that can be faked to manipulate weak people.

All of us must learn to manage our affections and love purely. There's no better checklist for the quality of our love than 1 Corinthians 13:4–7. It's worth reading every week: "Love is patient, love is kind. It does not envy, it does not boast, it is not proud. It is not rude, it is not self-seeking, it is not easily angered, it keeps no record of wrongs. Love does not delight in evil but rejoices with the truth. It always protects, always trusts, always hopes, always perseveres."

Again, there are no better environments in which to measure ourselves against this checklist than the family and the local church. In families and in churches, we have to learn purposefully to have healthy relationships both with people that we admire and people for whom we don't have a great deal of respect. "We 'like' or are 'fond of' some people, and not of others," wrote C. S. Lewis. "It is important to understand that this natural 'liking' is neither a sin nor a virtue, any more than your likes and dislikes in food are a sin or a virtue."[4] Love, in other words, is totally separate from how we happen to prefer one person to another. In order to express Christ's love and not bring dishonor to His name, we all must learn to maintain wholesome, healthy, holy relationships with a variety of people. It's what I call *managing our hearts*. If we change churches too often, we'll never learn the lesson. If we live alone, we won't learn the lesson. To love purely, we have to be with people.

What's more, we have to be with people over the long haul. True love achieves longevity. I believe it takes four years to really *meet* someone. In fact, I don't think actual ministry starts between most people for at least two years. Discipleship and genuine love are communicated in the midst of living life together over days and weeks and months and years. When I experience the divine flow toward someone, it's often an indication that God wants us to eventually do work together in His kingdom, but it may be several years before it actually happens.

Detecting and following God's divine flow is the way to follow and obey God in ministry. There is nothing but good things for our churches and our lives when we learn to follow the divine flow in our hearts.

Do you want to follow God? Then follow love.

Do you want to be guided by the Holy Spirit? Then be guided by love.

Wherever that stream of God's love flows out, follow it. I've sensed God's divine flow toward certain cities and have followed the divine flow by praying and giving toward the projects in those cities. I've sensed God's divine flow toward churches and have done what I could to help the people of those churches. And of course, I've sensed God's divine flow toward people, and have done all that I could to make the lives of those people better.

Let me repeat: "Love is intentionally doing something caring or helpful for another person, in Jesus' name, regardless of the cost or consequence to oneself." Don't be afraid of love, and don't let your ministry or church systems get in the way of love. God mends our hearts together with His love. He encourages lives with love. He works miracles by His love. So follow love! Be guided by love! Let the people in your church love one another according to God's plan.

I don't know of any ministry structure that encourages intentional love like free-market small groups. When we learn about love and begin to experience it, small groups form. People are so love starved that they will work, serve, or fly halfway around the world to do a love project with others they love for people they love. So when we say that God loves them and that His love in them will reach out toward others, they begin to experience the love of God and take action, and the ministry within a church can't help but expand. When people love their small groups, they won't have to be talked into attending their weekly meetings. When they love one another, they don't have to be reminded to take care of one another. When they love one another, they don't have to be coached on kindness and prayer. It naturally happens. It is, after all, love.

Near the end of *The Adventures of Tom Sawyer*, Tom and Huck stop for a break on their quest for buried treasure. Brimming with excitement over the possibilities of life, the two boys sit in the shade of an elm tree and shoot the breeze:

> "Say, Huck, if we find a treasure here, what you going to do with your share?"
>
> "Well, I'll have pie and a glass of soda every day, and I'll go to every circus that comes along . . ."
>
> " . . . What you going to do with yourn, Tom?"
>
> "I'm going to buy a new drum . . . and a red necktie and a bull pup, and get married."
>
> "Married!"
>
> "That's it."
>
> "Tom, you—why, you ain't in your right mind."
>
> "Wait—you'll see."
>
> " . . . What's the name of the gal?"
>
> " . . . I'll tell you sometime—not now."
>
> "All right—that'll do. Only if you get married I'll be more lonesomer than ever."
>
> "No, you won't. You'll come and live with me. Now stir out of this and we'll go to digging."[5]

CHAPTER TWELVE

Decent and in Order:
The Structure of Free-Market Small Groups

With Ted Whaley,
Director of Small-Group Ministry
at New Life Church

OK, AT THIS POINT IN THE BOOK YOU'VE GOT THE BASIC idea—you know what free-market small-group ministry can accomplish and why. For the remainder of the book, we're going to talk specifics. Practical application. In the chapters that follow, I'll tell you about the ten administrative pressures you don't have to worry about under the free-market small-group system, whether free-market small groups are right for your church and culture, and the nuts and bolts of how our system works at New Life.

I know that the free-market system sounds risky. I'm frequently asked, "How can an efficient church structure include beliefs in love and friendship and letting people develop wildly different small-group ideas?" But we have a very definite system in place. Order is important. Just as the free-market economy has a watchful government ensuring that it runs proficiently, a free-market church needs to understand how to make the system work so that it remains effective at serving people.

As I'll explain throughout the rest of the book, we have checks and balances in place for our small groups. We open the doors to all types of leaders, but you can be sure we know who those leaders are. Just because we believe leaders come in different shapes and sizes doesn't mean we don't examine leaders carefully. And while we appreciate the great wealth of ideas in our body of believers, we also know that some ideas are bad ideas. (Actually, incredibly pathetic!) We don't make people jump through hoops in order to lead a small group, but we do take appropriate measures to protect leaders, small-group members, and the church as a whole. As you'll see, our application process for new small-group leaders is fairly rigorous: it includes a personal interview, three references, an official State of Colorado background check, and the final approval of a pastor. We are careful to ensure that this process happens quickly and behind the scenes, but it does happen.

Also, though I believe discipleship happens naturally over the course of a strong, intentional relationship, I also believe that people need encouragement and accountability in order to remain intentional and forthright in their relationships. We don't impose an artificial accountability structure, but we do create an environment where accountability does happen. Every small-group leader enters into a relationship with a leader in authority over him or her, and those leaders have leaders, and even those leaders have leaders. (For all you C personalities out there, it's really quite impressive!)

There is no such thing as a secret among our leaders; communication is very open and honest, and if it's not, then it can become seemingly brutal. You've heard my arguments for love, friendship, and authenticity, but there are the deceivers, the manipulators, the control freaks, and the self-appointed teachers in the Body who would love to use our system for their own selfish purposes. We all know the realities of the old sin nature. So we emphasize 1 John 1:7 which says, "But if we walk in the light, as he is in the light, we have fellowship with one another, and the blood of Jesus, his Son, purifies us from all sin."

While there is a clear understanding of authority at New Life, we never give the impression that ministry is rocket science. Anyone can do it whose heart is open to the ministry of the Holy Spirit and who is willing to be discipled. People who are insubordinate or rebellious aren't successful in our system, but we're happy to work with leaders who make honest or ignorant mistakes. In fact, we're happiest when training someone to correct errors and serve Christ more effectively.

My fundamental belief is that God loves to work in people's lives. He calls all believers into ministry and wants to empower them to be effective in strengthening His kingdom. My job is to find a way to coach them in greater effectiveness, and the free-market small-group system has helped me do that like never before—it's open and flexible and life giving and exciting and challenging and fluid and dynamic, and it's also decent and in order.

UNDERSTANDING CHURCH MODELS

On the morning of September 11, 2001, I was sitting in the conference room of our church with our leadership team. We were, like most of America, glued to the television. The towers in New York had not yet fallen, the Pentagon was burning, and the plane had just crashed in Pennsylvania. The government was working to clear American airspace. We didn't know if the worst was over or if there was more terror to come, but I knew that the people of our church would be facing feelings of uncertainty and remorse in the coming weeks. Furthermore, I knew that the government might ask people not to gather in public places for a while—and even if they didn't, that people might be afraid to be in large groups.

Because Colorado Springs is the home to the Air Force Academy, NORAD, Peterson Air Force Base, and Fort Carson, we learned from church members working within the city that Colorado Springs was preparing to receive Air Force One if necessary. All the bases were sealed, the major roads within the city were barricaded, and the malls were evacuated. The governor ordered the Colorado National Guard to seal the airspace over the entire state, and we knew by the phone calls we were receiving from church members in the military and in the police forces that the government was prepared to take serious actions quickly.

I turned to Ted Whaley, our pastor of small-group ministry, and asked how long it would take to organize our nine thousand church members in house churches if it wasn't possible to meet together for a while. "Pastor Ted," he said, "we are ready now. If asked not to meet here in our building, we can have everyone in a house church within twenty-four hours. Sixty-five hundred New Lifers are already enrolled in small groups. The remaining members could be contacted and directed to a small group within seconds via phone, E-mail, or in person if necessary. Our neighborhood systems are in place." By early afternoon on September 11, 2001, the word was sent through the small-group chain of command about an all-church prayer meeting that evening, and we filled every seat in our auditorium that night!

I was impressed. Fortunately, we never had to activate those plans, but I realized that our church really was what I always hoped it would be: a facility-based church made up of small groups of individual believers who were living life together. Sundays at New Life aren't gatherings of thousands of individuals; they are gatherings of hundreds of small groups of people who know one another very well.

FOUR MODELS OF CHRISTIAN DISCIPLESHIP

There are four primary ways Christians group for discipleship, or have church.

1. Facility-Based Program Churches

This is the most common type of church we see in the free world—it's probably the type of church most of you reading this book work for or attend. Facility-based program churches have a building and they carry out their ministry to people through departments—the youth department, the music department, and so on. Each department runs a program that changes very little—if at all—from year to year. The leadership of these churches determines the types of ministries. If the senior pastor is the predominant authority, he has the final say on what the church does. If an elder board runs the church, their opinion takes precedence. In short, the church polity determines the ministry offerings in facility-based program churches. Facility-Based program churches are the largest in North America.

2. Facility-Based Cell Churches

A rapidly growing portion of the body of Christ is doing church this way. These churches have a building, but they carry out the majority of their ministry to people through their small-group system. The most popular of these is the classic cell system modeled by Yoido Full Gospel Church in Seoul, South Korea. Ralph Neighbor Jr. describes these traditional cell churches in his great books outlining the features of this system. Another type of cell system is from Bogotá, Colombia, which is the G-12 system. In this system, people are placed in groups of twelve in a pattern from the life of Christ and His disciples. This system, too, has been very effective in various places. There are other traditional cell models that you can learn about by going to this Web site: www.TouchUSA.org. Facility-based cell churches are the largest in the world.

3. Networks of House Churches

These networks function best in nations where facility-based churches are either tightly controlled by the government, or illegal. Networks of house churches are successful in Islamic and Communist countries because their success is reciprocal to the level of government control. These networks are trying to surface in Europe, where the state still funds churches. Such churches have been tried in the United States, but even where they've had some success, they've struggled in developing mission strategies and other projects that require coordinated, centralized effort. However, they are incredibly successful in nations where the government is trying to eliminate the Christian Church.

4. Free-Market Small-Group Churches

These are a combination of these first three models of ministry. Free-market small-group churches utilize the strongest elements of each of the other three systems to equip and mobilize Christians in ministry. Our church has a facility, and we believe it is very important to have a weekly meeting when we all gather to receive ministry from an apostle, prophet, evangelist, pastor, or teacher. We believe that since the pastor is the one with the primary spiritual responsibility in the local church, the pastor should speak most often, with the assistance of those who serve in other roles.

At church meetings, we receive common instruction, direction, and purpose in addition to having an opportunity to unite for worship and prayer and give tithes and offerings. During these services, we offer children's small groups that are similar to traditional Sunday school, as well as more traditional junior-high and adult services and classes. So on

Sundays, thousands of us gather strength from meeting together just as other facility-based churches do.

We also have the strength of the cell churches. As you know, our congregation is divided into smaller groups whose members know each other's names and families. They attend one another's weddings and funerals and visit one another in the hospital. They are involved in each other's lives in prayer, discipleship, Bible study, and in the fun areas of life like vacations, holiday celebrations, and evenings out together. These group members are forming a life history together.

The free-market small-group system also offers the strength of the networks of small groups. As I learned on September 11, we are set up so that if we ever need to convert to house networks, we can do so easily without missing a step.

FREE-MARKET MINISTRY IN A SMALL CHURCH

All of the successful small group/cell churches that I know of started as program-based churches. As a matter of fact, New Life was a pure facility-based program church until we reached 4,800 people. Actually, I don't know of any large cell-based churches that were planted as cell churches. All of the ones I'm aware of worldwide were facility-based program churches that transitioned once they were in the thousands. So I encourage churches with fewer than 200 people and newly planted churches to focus on developing a corporate identity through strong, successful weekend services and traditional program-based ministry. A group of 200 can successfully connect with each other and be discipled through the traditional ministry programs of a small church. If nothing else, they will connect in a healthy way through the teamwork it takes to get a church off the ground and into a growth mode—teaching Sunday School, cleaning the church building, ushering, providing nursery services, staffing information tables, preparing communion, providing altar ministries, and things like these. All of these natural groupings can be effective connecting points for people and still maintain a common focus on developing and strengthening the church's corporate identity of main services. So in effect these types of functional ministry groups are the church's small groups. When churches of 200 or less organize their congregation into smaller groups with disparate focuses, they often lose momentum and sometimes lose the church entirely. Thus, I don't recommend traditional cells for churches of 200 or fewer.

Somewhere around the 200-member benchmark, the demands on the pastors and church leaders start increasing exponentially. It only takes a crisis in the life of one member to require all of our time for a while, which may leave the balance of the congregation wanting. This, along with the other demands of ministry and pastoral care, crossing the 200-member line brings a multiplication of activities. More people means more moving parts, which puts a significant strain on traditional program-based systems.

I believe the busiest pastors are those who pastor congregations of 150 to 250 people. At this size, there isn't a great deal of money for staff to undergird the ministry to the congregation. Thus, pastors in this size congregation are counselors, business leaders, therapists, friends, coaches, Bible scholars, teachers, and entertainers. Very often pastors in this size church find themselves in the quagmire of juxtaposed interests in their congregations. And unfortunately, the pastors of these churches find their spouses working in various support positions for the church and leaving their children struggling for attention because of the demands of the church upon their parents.

No doubt, the diversity of needs coming to your attention from members can feel overwhelming. At this point, the staff of a small church can start to feel overwhelmed trying to keep spinning all the plates of the needs of a growing congregation.

This doesn't need to be. It's terrible that such good people find themselves stretched so thin because of the structure of their church. I know that the appearance is that the demands of ministry stretch the resources of the church and ministers, but it's not true. There are plenty of resources, but if they become unfocused (traditional cells in a small church) or centered on one person (program-based church with most of the ministry responsibilities on the senior Pastor) and then the church will probably stagnate.

Over the years of pastoring, I've stumbled onto a fundamental truth: Our average members—the soccer mom and the plumber and the schoolteacher—have a pretty good sense of the needs in the Body. Even better than my staff and I do, they know what people are thinking and feeling, what they like, prefer, and respond to—what they need. No doubt, in a church of 200 people there are some built-in commonalities among people. And undoubtedly, these areas of common interest will make great ministry.

But first the move to free-market ministry has to focus on strengthening the infrastructure of the church as a whole. So what does this mean? The ushers become a small group with a purpose that transcends—but still includes—greeting people and collecting the offering. Now the people who like to serve in this way have a forum to form healthy intentional relationships. The head usher becomes the small-group leader. Simple things like coffee and bagels together thirty minutes before the service, with a little time to interact with each other and pray before serving together, are building blocks for healthy relationships.

The same idea can be applied to the other tasks that have to be performed to maintain the core function of the church. The choir can be divided into small groups. Sunday school teachers can be formed into small groups. You'll find that the more connected these people feel, the more committed to their task they will be—and the more they will enjoy it!

Once the existing ministries and programs understand that an additional benefit of their service to the church is the opportunity to connect with people, you'll quickly be able to identify other small-group ministry opportunities that connect people: the guys who meet at the coffee shop on Tuesday mornings, the women who gather for Bible study around the kitchen table on Thursday afternoons, the couples who serve Communion, the college students who meet at the park for a pickup game on Saturday afternoon . . . these are all ready-made small groups just waiting to be empowered as part of the church's ministry. All of these people will be encouraged when you make them leaders, and in no time will be influencing the lives of other members of your church and those outside your congregation in the community.

One significant note about this stage: You don't have to do much except say "Yes." People in the congregation will have ideas and desires that will minister to others and connect people in the community. So when they mention them to you, direct them to small-group leader training. When they ask you permission, tell them "Yes" if it's at all reasonable. You'll find your church mobilizing people in ministry and naturally changing from a church solely dependent upon the pastor for ministry to a church being empowered by the pastor and the professional ministry team. The power of lay ministry will cause the church to grow, and the 200 barrier will be naturally overcome while, at the same time, the church will transition into a small-group church by saying "yes" and providing direction to those who want to serve.

It will happen naturally and quickly. Before you know it your people will be ministering to the Body and to the community, all under the banner of your church. You can casually tell the congregation that they are all called to be ministers, and that you are there to equip them without making an issue of it or discouraging those who have already been serving faithfully in the programs of the church. Once you offer an invitation for people to develop their ministries around their interests, their gifts, and their passions, you will be amazed at how quickly and easily it will happen. This chapter gives you an idea of the structure to build on, and the chapter titled "Nuts and Bolts" will provide some very specific tools that can be easily adapted to a church of any size. The key is to let ministry develop from the ground up. You don't have to tear your hair out coming up with new programs and catchy ideas to try to get people in. Over the last few years many churches have adapted this concept for building their ministry—all with the same positive results.

Most recently, a church in Monterey, California—a church of about two hundred people—asked us to help them develop free-market small-group ministry. Up to this point they had eight small groups. After they rearranged their thinking and opened up the gates to free-market small groups, they immediately grew to thirty-five small groups! That's real church growth!

THE CONVERSION
TO THE FREE-MARKET SYSTEM

When we reached fifteen hundred members, we implemented what I call Sermon Cells. These cells were made up of three to twelve people in homes and businesses, and meetings were to last no more than two hours. The participants had snacks and perhaps an icebreaker, and then studied notes that provided a more in-depth examination of the subject that had been covered in the previous Sunday's sermon. We did all we could to make these cells work, and they worked OK for those who attended. But as I explained in detail earlier, most of the participants were either A+ people or the most needy people. The majority of our church body wasn't interested in attending, or was too busy to attend.

I worked hard on these cells. We learned all we could from Neighbor, Hayford, Stockstill, Cho, Khong, and others who were well-known in the cell-church world. I preached on the subject, and was happy with the results in the lives of those who participated. But we couldn't get a large enough percentage of our congregation to participate. At our largest point, we had eighty cells that were serving our congregation.

In order to minister to the whole church, we had to resurrect our facility-based program model and relegate cells to a department along with the other departments of our church. (Which, I might add, is exactly where many churches in the United States who have tried cells have settled. They are program churches with one extra program—youth, music, children, adult, and cells.)

As I've explained, I soon became convinced that there had to be a better way to mobilize the incredible ministries within the church that were not being utilized. Many people had ideas for ministry, but it was too much work to implement their ideas. It required too many people's approval, a budget, a place for ministry to be arranged, and a staff. Because of these difficulties, most of the ideas for ministry from our congregation received, in effect, a "No."

While we were dealing with these issues, some of us from the New Life staff attended a conference at Tommy Barnett's First Assembly of God Church in Phoenix, Arizona. At one meeting we learned that Pastor Barnett's church had 150 ministries run by different people in his church. It struck me that these ministries were accomplishing the objectives that cell groups were supposed to accomplish in a large church with one added benefit—they were ministry task groups. I called them "cell groups with a purpose." I know that traditional cells have a very important purpose, but I loved that Pastor Barnett had provided an opportunity for the people in his church to reach out and serve the church and the community through a group with a common objective.

No one else referred to them as cells or small groups, but those within the ministries learned one another's names, became accountable to one another, and discipled one another in the midst of their ministry tasks. The application was shouting at me. They were great expressions of God's love. And I knew why the members of First Assembly loved these ministries so much: They appealed to their own interests.

With Barnett's model in mind, we added one fundamental principle: that the people within the church have good ideas about how to disciple the people they know in the community. They, the people, are the source of good ideas for ministry. I had been looking for a way to say "Yes" to the people we had been saying "No" to, and now I knew I had it. If people had a good idea for ministry, free-market small groups would give them an opportunity to try it out. If it worked, fantastic. If not, the group would die out naturally and they could try something else.

Meanwhile, we could keep everything that was working in our traditional cells, and we could begin to add additional cells that were focused around ministries that the people in the church wanted to try. We could keep the structures that were already in place. The free-market system wasn't going to mess anything up. It wasn't going to ruin accountability relationships or impede discipleship. In fact, in time we learned that it encouraged them. We'd still have capable leaders in place, and we'd train them to be effective. We didn't yet know how it would all work, but we felt sure that we could start the system and let it run while ensuring that everything was decent and in order.

So, how did we start? It was easy. We didn't ever announce to anyone that we were changing our system. Nor did we tell them that we were launching into a new philosophy of ministry. We simply provided a structure to enable them to do what we had been saying all along:

- We had been saying that they were all ministers.

- We had been saying that God had a call on their lives.

- We had been saying that they had natural ministry opportunities with their friends and loved ones.

- We had been saying that they were in relationships for a reason.

Now, with the introduction of free-market small groups, we simply implemented a system to help them do what we had been saying they could do.

When I introduced it, I didn't make a big deal out of it. I didn't even really tell them what we were doing—I didn't say, "We have decided to make our church a free-market small-group church." Instead, I stood in front of the congregation and told them that our church was incredibly healthy, which it was. Then I said that I knew that many of them had wonderful ministries within them, and that if they would like to join with the sermon cell leaders for training and assistance, we would be delighted to serve with them. I asked everyone who wanted to be a small-group leader to come to a four-hour orientation session on Sunday afternoon. We immediately had more than a hundred new people wanting to start ministry small groups.

That brought a transition. Our small groups have increased in number every fall and spring semester since, and we've continued to develop systems of checks and balances to make sure everything runs properly. It wasn't difficult. The church barely noticed we were doing anything different. But the volume and quantity of ministry to our church body and our community began to expand significantly.

That, in fact, is the grand beauty of this system. Without anyone noticing, we fundamentally and radically strengthened and improved our church. All of our departments are still in place, but they function as small-group sections. We have children's small groups, junior-high and high-school small groups, and college-age small groups. We have small groups for singles, married couples, men, women, and seniors. The purpose of every department in the church is to provide encouragement for connecting, discipleship, and outreach.

SIX REASONS TO SAY "YES"

I never dreamed people would be so creative and innovative. Now if people want to teach a Bible study, I say "Yes." If they want to teach some Christian book they appreciate, I can say "Yes." If they want to teach C. S. Lewis, lead prayer, or minister in power ministries, I can say "Yes." I know some of you are saying, "How can you say 'Yes'? You are opening Pandora's box. How can you control it? How can you ensure quality? Who watches these folks?"

I can say "Yes" because of six things. I'll explain all these in more detail later, but I'll give you an overview now so you can see the basic structure of the ministry.

First, every potential small-group leader must go through the four-hour Small-Group Leader Orientation. We offer this class three times a year and usually have more than a hundred new people taking the class. During this afternoon session, they learn about the authority structure, the level of commitment required, and the basic theology of our church. They learn that they have to be willing to teach this theology if they are to be approved as small-group leaders.

Second, to finalize their small groups, people need to meet with a section leader, zone leader, or district leader (you will learn about these in "Nuts and Bolts"). In these sessions, the leaders either help them refine the basic idea or encourage them to attend some other small groups before beginning their own.

Third, during the approval process to be a small-group leader, candidates are given DISC and Gift-Quest tests so they can identify their own personality profiles and spiritual gifts. This helps them refine their direction in ministry.

Fourth, if they want to teach something they have read or a curriculum with which they are familiar, their section leader must approve that material.

Fifth, once a new small-group leader begins, his section leader is responsible to attend the small group periodically to ensure that the new leader is growing in his role.

Sixth, all small-group leaders, old and new, are required to attend ongoing training each month.

This might sound like a lot, but it's not. These are very easy rules and encouraging steps that the new leaders enjoy. It makes things safe for us by giving us a few ways to check on the people applying for leadership and make sure they know that they must stick to the Statement of Faith. It's enough to provide peace of mind for both us and them, but not enough to discourage them. And it helps me say "Yes," because it gives us a basic process to guarantee that we're getting quality leaders we'll be able to coach through our existing leadership.

I've found that good Christians don't want to do anything that displeases their senior pastor. So when they know that I am fully supportive of their ministries, it is an emotional and spiritual catalyst. It's incredible how much people want permission to do the right thing. When I say, "Go for it!" or "That sounds like a great idea" or "You would make a great small-group leader," they are energized to give it a shot. Sometimes I'll remind them, "Look, this is a unique idea, so let's try it. If it works, great. If not, at least we tried." Then they know they don't have to do everything perfectly, but they still have the support and understanding from their pastor.

It works. It's safe. It's effective. It will revolutionize your church.

CHAPTER THIRTEEN

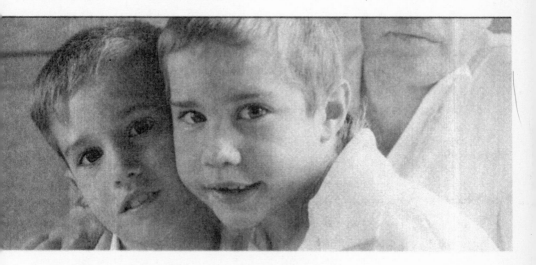

Are Free-Market Small Groups Right for You?

With Russ Walker,
Senior Pastor of Community Church
in Whitewater, Wisconsin

WELL, WHAT DO YOU THINK? I'VE TOLD YOU HOW SMALL groups work and why I think the free-market small-group system should be considered by most churches. We've talked about how people naturally group, about embracing individuality, about the power of love and friendship, and why churches should be permission granting. We've discussed how there is still a fundamental structure in the free-market system to ensure accountability, discipleship, and correct theology, and we've outlined how the structure helps ease some of the pressures most churches face. Once you read through the nuts and bolts of our system, you'll have everything you need to begin developing the power of free-market ideas in your church or ministry.

But does this mean you should do it? It depends. Earlier in the book, we talked about how different churches have used a wide variety of small-group systems with great success, and that churches should weigh the different variables when choosing a small-group system. The personality of the pastor, culture of the church, and whether or not the community has endured significant suffering are important dynamics to consider. Small groups are necessary no matter what your church is like, but different types of small groups will work to varying degrees from place to place.

Outside of America, it's not uncommon to see churches with thousands and even tens of thousands of small groups. When we first studied the various small-group models, we found La Misión Cristiana Elim (MCE) in San Salvador, El Salvador, which at that time had 12,000 cell groups. That was small compared to Dion Robert's church in Ivory Coast, which now has approximately 18,000 groups, or César Castellanos's church in Colombia of 14,000 groups (now with approximately 20,000 groups). Dr. Cho's Yoido Full Gospel Church in South Korea had more than over 14,000 groups at that time. (They now have approximately 20,000.) With those figures in mind, it was hard not to be a little disappointed when our first small-group system at New Life yielded less than one hundred groups. We were pleased with what was happening to some extent, but we never had the sense that our whole church was embracing the idea of small groups, and the vast majority of our members weren't becoming involved.

But as I said earlier, we soon realized that we'd never have success by simply replicating what other churches were doing. We had to do something that made sense in Colorado Springs, Colorado. We had to find something that would work here.

And you've got to find something that will work for you too. If the model you need doesn't yet exist, create it. In doing so, you'll be capitalizing on the power of the free-market system, but that doesn't mean your free-market structure needs to look exactly like ours. That's the genius of the free market: Change is inevitable, growth is unlimited, and there's no pressure to stick to any one way of doing things. Do whatever works. Make it happen. Find a way to connect people in the body of Christ and help expand the kingdom of God.

THE ABSOLUTES OF ANY SMALL-GROUP SYSTEM

Of course, there are fundamental principles that apply to all churches that are intentionally connecting people through small groups. Remember the earlier discussion of absolutes, interpretations, deductions, and personal preferences? Well, there are some absolutes regarding the ways people connect in small groups. My team and I have watched many churches struggle with the implementation of small-group ministry, and every time the problem is either that the church has simply chosen the wrong model, or they haven't adhered to the following seven absolutes.

1. The Senior Pastor Must Be Involved

For any small-group ministry to be effective, the senior pastor must participate. He doesn't have to administer the ministry but he must believe in the ministry and get behind it 100 percent. I stay in close contact with our primary small-group pastor, and I help in the training at the Small-Group Leader Orientation each semester. Perhaps most importantly, I champion small groups from the platform and whenever talking with New Lifers. One of my highest priorities as Senior Pastor of New Life Church is to assist the small-group ministry however I can. Any church that wants to have a thriving small-group ministry needs a senior pastor who appreciates, supports, and believes in the power of small groups.

2. The Church Must Be Based on Small Groups, Not Big Programs

A couple of years ago, our small-group ministry's motto was "Think Small." We spattered the saying on church walls, T-shirts, buttons, and flyers. We were trying to create a paradigm shift in our church: The point isn't big meetings; the point is small groups of people living life together. That's discipleship. That's the purpose of the church.

We still have large meetings for youth, college, singles, and others, but we emphasize that these meetings are gatherings of small groups. We have big Sunday meetings for special emphasis and use Christmas and Easter to draw tens of thousands to special productions. Massive meetings can help motivate people in ministry, but actual discipleship begins when they connect in a smaller setting. Thus, the big meetings are there for the purpose of connecting people to God and to smaller groups.

People aren't just choosing small groups among the variety of church programs. We schedule weekly meetings so that they don't compete with small groups. We have created a small-group culture within our church. The small-group ministry isn't just like the youth ministry or the praise-and-worship ministry. Rather, those ministries are sections of small groups. We are a small-group church.

3. The Church Must Adhere to the Ephesians 4 Model

Churches are too much work when they are based entirely on the senior pastor. Sure, lots of people might come to hear a good speaker, but genuine success is a question of how well a church enables its members to become effective ministers. Ephesians 4:11–12 reminds us that God uses apostles, prophets, evangelists, pastors, and teachers for a very specific purpose: "to prepare God's people for works of service, so that the body of Christ may be built up." The senior pastor of a small-group church has to be effective at empowering people for works of service. His ministry is helping them find their ministries.

For many pastors, this is easier said than done. All of us have a tendency to just do it all ourselves so we can make sure it's done the way we want it to be done. But we have to relinquish that control so that true multiplication of ministry can happen throughout the church. Being called to be a pastor (or, for that matter, an apostle, prophet, evangelist, or teacher) means being called to serve people by helping them fulfill God's calling on their lives.

4. Tiers of Leadership Must Be Established

For effective coaching and accountability in small-group ministry, there must be tiered levels of leadership. I've mentioned this before, and we'll discuss what this looks like at New Life in the next chapter. Every five to eight small-group leaders need to have a coach (section leader). Every five to ten section leaders need to have a coach (zone leader). And every five to ten zone leaders need to have a coach (district leader).

Many small-group churches make the mistake of assigning one person to lead the entire small-group ministry. There's no way one person can effectively disciple a large number of people in a close and consistent manner. Every church needs a system in which every leader has someone he or she can talk to and no one feels overwhelmed with too much responsibility.

5. Outline Clear Responsibilities and Expectations

When leaders burn out, it's often because they aren't sure of their expectations—generally, they're doing much more than is really required. Provide job descriptions and time requirements so that each level of leader knows what they are committing to. People need to be able to count the cost before they make a commitment.

6. Conduct a Simple Initial Orientation

When dealing with new small-group leaders, you should have an initial orientation so they can learn about the church's philosophy of ministry. You don't need to cover every issue of leadership, but trainees should feel as though they have had an introduction to the ministry and can feel comfortable with the expectations and responsibilities of their leadership positions. It is during initial orientation that potential leaders will complete their applications, background checks, and personality profiles, and go through their interviews. Once a potential leader has gone through the initial orientation and the application has been approved, the participant is eligible to become a small-group leader.

Why is this an absolute? Because it accomplishes several things that many small-group ministries struggle with: It provides an opportunity for you to formally examine potential leaders, but without any awkwardness, inefficiency, or pressure; it helps people know up front whether or not they really want to commit to leadership; and it gives incoming leaders a complete understanding of what their leadership positions will look like.

7. Conduct Ongoing Job Training

Ongoing training is extremely important. It takes continual training to equip people for ministry and fulfill the Ephesians 4 model. At New Life, small-group leaders go to training meetings once a month, and the leaders over them coach them even more regularly. Making the training process easy and doable doesn't mean minimizing training. The training of small-group leaders at New Life is far and away one of the major advantages of our small-group ministry. As word gets out about how great the training is, more people want to be leaders so they can receive the quality training.

STARTING TO CHOOSE
A SMALL-GROUP SYSTEM

OK, so you know you want to do small groups, you're prepared to follow the absolutes, and you're ready to choose a system. Now, it's time to think through the ideas I've been alluding to throughout this book: the culture of your city, the culture of your church, the personality of the senior pastor, and the level of involvement of the senior pastor. Consider the following:

What is the culture of your city?

- ❏ transient
- ❏ permanent residents
- ❏ retired community
- ❏ military community
- ❏ family community
- ❏ singles community
- ❏ white-collar community
- ❏ blue-collar community
- ❏ large population
- ❏ medium population
- ❏ small population
- ❏ high percentage of believers
- ❏ medium percentage of believers
- ❏ low percentage of believers

What is the culture of your church?

1. Identify all of the different cultures that currently exist within your church.

2. Are there any cultures in your church that are in direct opposition to a small-group culture?

What is the personality of the senior pastor? (DISC profile)

❏ D: dominant, driven, determined, direct, decisive

❏ I: influencing, inspiring, impulsive, enthusiastic, talkative

❏ S: stable, steady, sensitive, sympathetic, sincere

❏ C: correct, compliant, conscientious, careful, detailed

What level of participation/leadership does the senior pastor want to take in the small-group ministry?

❏ High: wants to personally lead the small-group ministry. Wants to have a hand in training and motivating leaders. Treats this ministry as the most important ministry in the church. In fact, this is the ministry of the church.

❏ Mid: believes in small groups but wants someone else to lead the small-group ministry. May do some leadership training from time to time but delegates the majority of the responsibility to someone else. Treats this ministry as one of the most important ministries of the church but needs to juggle it with some of the other important ministries of the church.

❏ Low: passively agrees to have small groups as part of the ministry in the church but doesn't want to be bothered by any of the responsibilities. Will treat this ministry like any other ministry in the church.

In the following section, we'll analyze how churches can choose from different small-group models according to how they answer the previous questions. First, let's look at a few of the models.

FOUR MODELS OF SMALL GROUPS

There are four types of small-group models that are very effective in the United States: the Pure Cell Model popularized by Ralph Neighbor, the

Combination Cell Model popularized by Dale Galloway, the G-12 Cell Model popularized by Larry Stockstill, and the Free-Market Small-Group Model popularized by me.

1. Pure Cell Model

Definition: The Pure Cell Model mandates that small groups never grow larger than fifteen people; they multiply as they reach this figure. There are no (or very few) church activities other than cell groups. Everything in the church is an extension of the cells and flows from their combined strength. This model incorporates building long-term relationships with discipleship that is done in an organized, focused, and centralized way, and all groups study the same thing. It also stresses reaching out to unbelievers. This model appeals to people who want long-term relationships and security and to people who want to be discipled.

Advantages: All of the small groups are doing the same thing, which allows for continuity and a single focus. This minimizes the risk of leaders covering material that is contrary to the beliefs of the church. The small groups are discussion-oriented, which makes them conducive for discipleship. They are also conducive to long-term relationships and allow for effective pastoral care.

Disadvantages: Pure cells are not useful for leaders who have a gift of teaching because, first, leaders are encouraged to *lead* discussions rather than teach. Further, the number and type of leaders are limited to those who are comfortable teaching the church's prescribed material. Finally, with pure cells, the groups must divide or break into two groups once they reach a certain number of participants. This can break up relationships for the sake of growth.

How are relationships built? People join a group based primarily on the location of the group and secondarily on the people they know. People are connected through relationships; however, they might need to separate due to multiplication.

How is discipleship done? Leaders conduct group discussions and one-on-one sessions based on the material they've been trained to use.

How is evangelism done? Each person in a "shepherd group" is encouraged to bring an unbelieving friend to a "share group."

How is multiplication achieved? The group is split into two groups as it approaches fifteen people. There is a strong emphasis on raising up assistant leaders to lead new groups as members multiply.

How many people are in a group? No more than fifteen.

What is the commitment for small group members? Open-ended.

What is its fundamental premise? Every need that a person has can be met in one small group.

Unique features: Groups are all covering the same material, and each group is encouraged to reproduce itself through multiplication.

2. Combination Cell Model

Definition: The Combination Cell Model incorporates principles of multiplication, relationship building, and evangelism from the Pure Cell Model. What differentiates this model is the way it handles discipleship. In the Pure Cell Model, the premise is that every need can be met in the small group. In the Combination Cell Model, the premise is that most needs can be met in a small group, but that there are some specific areas that should be emphasized for more effective discipleship to occur. Therefore, focus groups are introduced. These are smaller groups that concentrate a group of people on a specific topic. So small groups and focus groups together make up the small-group ministry. This model appeals to people who want to form long-term relationships but also have a need in a certain area.

Advantages: This approach combines the advantages of a Pure Cell Model with the addition of focus groups that deal with particular issues. For example, men's, women's, singles', and seniors' ministries can be emphasized through focus groups. Another advantage of this model is that it allows for leaders who have a gift of teaching to express their gift (groups can consist of discussions or teachings).

Disadvantages: The focus groups complicate the model by having several foci instead of just one, which can lead to a competition between focus groups and small groups.

How are relationships built? This is done in ways similar to the Pure Cell Model, with the addition of focus groups offering the opportunity for people to meet others of like interests or needs.

How is discipleship done? Discipleship is achieved in the same way as in the Pure Cell Model, with the addition of focus groups doing specific discipleship on specific topics.

How is evangelism done? Evangelism is done similar to the way the Pure Cell Model does it, with the addition of having focus groups that may have a specific appeal to unbelievers.

How is multiplication achieved? Small groups are split just as in the Pure Cell Model, but focus groups have a starting and stopping point.

How many people are in a group? Most groups have fifteen or less, but a few can have more.

What is the commitment for small-group members? Most are open-ended, but the focus groups may have a definite starting and stopping point.

What is its fundamental premise? The small group can meet most needs; however, there are some unique needs that must be met by a focus group.

Unique features: This model combines elements from the Pure Cell Model with the Free-Market Small-Group Model.

3. G-12 Cell Model

Definition: The G-12 Cell Model is based on the idea that Jesus particularly picked twelve men to disciple. Each group begins with twelve new people; each of those twelve will eventually form another group of twelve. Long-term relationships are built because the group never separates. Each person is discipled with the intent that he or she will also become a discipler. Multiplication occurs when a person in a group starts a group in which he or she is the leader and begins to build a new group of twelve. So the intent is for every person to be a disciple and to be a discipler. Each group determines its own topics. This model appeals to people who want to build long-term relationships and who want to develop a sense of community and belonging.

Advantages: This model builds strong relationships without the threat of the relationships being split up due to multiplication. It is very effective for pastoral care. It also emphasizes the need to be discipled, but with an equal emphasis on the need for each person to disciple others. The G-12 Model allows for a variety of topics, issues, and emphases to be the focal point of the group.

Disadvantages: This model can generate the feeling that its groups are lifelong groups with no ending point. Hence, the G-12 Model is not conducive to transient communities. Furthermore, it takes time to generate momentum because this model is contrary to the average American lifestyle. Finally, it can be very time-consuming to maintain this style of small-group ministry.

How are relationships built? People join a group primarily because of existing relationships; they then recruit others to be a part of that group. Relationships are long-term.

How is discipleship done? Discipleship is accomplished in the same manner as in the Pure Cell Model.

How is evangelism done? Evangelizing for this model is done through the principle of being discipled until you become a discipler. Each person is encouraged to bring an unbelieving friend to his or her group.

How is multiplication achieved? Each member of a group is discipled until that person can lead a group independently with people he or she recruits.

How many people are in a group? Up to twelve, plus the leader.

What is the commitment for small-group members? Open-ended.

What is its fundamental premise? Jesus discipled twelve people who then in turn discipled others.

Unique features: Every person is challenged to be in two groups, to be led and to be a leader.

4. Free-Market Small-Group Model

Definition: In the Free-Market Small-Group Model, the number of people in each group is not limited, but left up to the ability of the leader and the interest of the people. Emphasis is given to meeting the felt needs and/or interests of people; therefore, a multitude of topics and interests is available. People choose the type of group they want to go to based on relationships or an interest or need they might have. There are clear starting and stopping points in this model, so people sign up for a group knowing the commitment beforehand. Because it is a free-market system, the best groups are the ones that survive; the weaker groups dissolve. This model has a high appeal to the independence bred into members of a free-market culture.

Advantages: The Free-Market Small-Group Model offers broad-based ministry to people of all spiritual levels—in the church body and the local community. Groups in this model focus on meeting people's felt needs. Leaders are given the latitude to express their gifts in areas that are appealing to them, which increases the leadership availability pool.

Finally, there is an obvious starting and stopping point, so people know what they are committing to before they commit.

Disadvantages: In this model, there is greater risk of leaders covering material that is contrary to the beliefs of the church. Worse, if not taught correctly, this model can lead to the promotion of short-term, superficial relationships. There is also an increase in the administrative concerns of this model due to the stopping and starting points and the multitude of small-group choices.

How are relationships built? People join a group primarily because of similar interests or felt needs. Relationships might be short-term but have the potential to become long-term.

How is discipleship done? People are discipled by joining a group that meets a specific felt need. It is left up to the individual to decide which group to be a part of.

How is evangelism done? Because of the variety of the groups and the short-term time commitment, every members is encouraged to invite an unbelieving friend to a group that would appeal to him. The wide variety of small groups offered appeals to nonbelievers outside the church (e.g., hiking, oil painting, etc.).

How is multiplication achieved? Each person is encouraged to bring a friend, but often the group topic creates a natural draw. The beginning of a new segment of groups causes a natural multiplication. Larger groups develop assistant leaders to offer additional like-kind groups in future semesters.

How many people are in a group? Every small group must have a minimum of three participants. There is no maximum limit.

What is the commitment for small-group members? All of the groups have a specific starting and stopping point.

What is its fundamental premise? People join small groups primarily because of a felt need or shared interest.

Unique features: The year is broken into segments during which the groups function. People sign up for a particular group at the beginning of each segment based on their own felt needs or interests.

When we adopted free-market small groups at New Life, the people of our church responded. I believe the free-market model will work in almost any church if the correct variables are in. But again, each church has to choose the system that will work the best for it. It's vital for the body of

Christ to connect in a powerful, life-giving way, and we should do whatever it takes to figure out how to make that happen in our area. God wants His Body to be a growing, healthy family of believers, and I think He's happiest when we're learning how to make that family work.

Chapter Fourteen

Nuts and Bolts

With Ted Whaley,
Director of Small-Group Ministry
at New Life Church

A COUPLE OF YEARS AGO A WOMAN IN OUR CHURCH FORMED A small group based on something she had wanted to do all of her life. From as early as she could remember, she had wanted to learn how to be a circus clown. She didn't know if anyone else would find the idea interesting at all, but she started a group called "Clowning Around" for the purposes of learning how to apply clown makeup, constructing clown costumes, and learning clown tricks to spread the gospel in a new and different way. The response was huge. Today, two "Clowning Around" small groups average about twenty-five to thirty people each semester. They started by serving the children's ministry at New Life, but they soon expanded to city parks, parades, and festivals throughout Colorado Springs.

No one on our pastoral staff would ever have thought of a clown ministry, but the free-market system created an environment in which this woman could pursue her idea, and God has used her desire to minister to hundreds of kids and adults in our community.

I've said it before and I'll say it again (and keep saying it for the rest of my life): Our purpose as a church is to be life-giving. That means that we promote life, not death, to everyone in our sphere of influence. That means we champion people. That means we don't control or prohibit—we say "Yes!" We don't create hurdles; we open doors. We don't determine who belongs arbitrarily; we strategize to include as many people as possible. We don't serve systems or particular models of ministry; we serve people. We are successful only when we are empowering people to do the life-giving ministry that God has called them to do.

DEFINING THE STRUCTURE

I like our system to be as open and flexible as possible in order to serve the people in it, but there is a definite and necessary structure to it. It is a moveable system, but it is a system. Particularly as a church grows, it's imperative to have levels of leaders, to know how to administer, and to be prepared to meet requests and coach people through problems. We've designed and redesigned our free-market small-group system very carefully, and we continue to tweak it every year. In this chapter, I'll describe the basic nuts and bolts that make it work.

Leadership System: Sections, Zones, and Districts

Only three years ago, "Marriage Ministry" at New Life Church consisted of pastors counseling couples in crisis, perhaps a big event focused on marriage each year, and two or three marriage-related small groups. Martin and Aileen Rediger and Tim and Meg Britton led two of those groups—both had strong marriages, a track record for helping other couples, and a passion to strengthen marriages. Out of their passion for couples, they began to encourage others in leadership.

Before we knew it, we had an entire section of marriage-related small groups under Martin and Aileen's care as section leaders. Today, Martin and Aileen and Tim and Meg are zone leaders overseeing four sections of marriage-related groups for couples at every stage of life. Under direction of the Redigers and the Brittons, almost every area related to marriage is covered. When we host a citywide marriage seminar, these folks step up to the plate and take care of everything—with enthusiasm and passion! That's the way it happens with every area of free-market small-group ministry—it starts at the bottom and grows—no, it explodes.

There are three tiers of leadership in the small-group system at New Life: sections, zones, and districts. We designed it this way to provide an intimate spiritual covering for our leaders and to make it possible to do what God has called them to do.

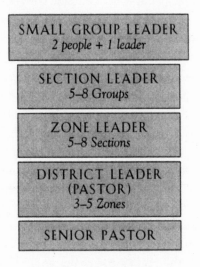

Sections. A section consists of five to eight small groups that are (usually) similar in nature. Every small group has a leader, and every section of small groups also has a leader. The section leader and the small-group leader have a critical relationship. Each section leader meets with every small-group leader in his or her section on a regular basis. This forms the principal discipling relationship for every small-group leader. Section leaders are people who have successfully led small groups. They visit one of the small groups in their section at least once every semester. In addition, they stay in personal contact with all of the leaders in their section over the phone or by E-mail, or at coffee or lunch meetings.

Zones. Five to eight sections create a zone, and every zone has a leader. As with the small-group leader/section-leader relationship, the zone-leader/section-leader relationship is crucial to both the success of every section and to the success of every section leader. The zone leaders, of course, are also people who have had experience in leading good small groups, and they also stay in contact with the leaders in their zones. In addition, zone leaders help assess the overall direction of training and are actively involved in coaching leaders.

Districts. Three to five zones make up a district, and every district has a staff pastor from New Life. Again, discipleship develops out of relationship. Our district pastors oversee the zones of groups in which they have a passion for ministry. Some of our zones coincide with our traditional church departments, such as youth ministry, children's ministry, and so on.

How do we decide when to add new sections, zones, and districts? It depends entirely upon what the market dictates. We don't create them; we let the market create them naturally. Several years ago a woman named Rose decided to start a small group called "Beginning Guitar." She wanted to teach people to play the guitar using worship music. She had been concerned that no one would come to her group, but on the first night, forty-seven people showed up at her home! She called the church in panic the next day—it was great that so many people wanted to learn, but this was hardly a "small" group! Where would they all park? How could they all fit in her house?

We quickly mobilized her section leader to work on the problem, and they moved the group to the church for the rest of the semester. Rose also immediately began trying to identify assistant leaders who could help her facilitate the group. By the end of the semester, 107 were coming to the group on a regular basis. Rose was able to teach a basic lesson to everyone and then split the group into smaller groups for the bulk of the evening.

The next semester, the people who had assisted Rose stepped up to form their own guitar small groups, and we suddenly had a whole section of groups for guitar players. There were basic, intermediate, and advanced guitar small groups. I never would have dreamed that I'd lead a church where one of the biggest sections of small groups had to do with playing guitar, but that's what happened because that's what the market dictated. In the free-market system, people vote with their feet. Growth and multiplication happen naturally, and the system adjusts to meet the demand.

The Entry Point

The entry point for a person who wants to be a small-group leader is the orientation meeting I described earlier. Halfway into each semester, we conduct a Small-Group Leader Orientation class on a Sunday afternoon from 1:00 to 5:00 P.M. We start announcing it a few weeks beforehand, telling people we'll provide lunch and child care. We do it right after the last Sunday-morning service so people won't go home for naps or sports, and we make sure they know it's strictly an *orientation*, not a recruitment session. The people who come aren't required to become small-group leaders—this is an opportunity for them to get to know the system. The people coming to this meeting are not recruited, and they are not obligated to become small-group leaders.

During the orientation, we talk about principles of leadership and the biblical basis for small groups. There's plenty of time for people to ask questions and have their concerns addressed. I explain the idea that a small-group leader is a pastor to the people in his or her group. I also outline the basic tenets in our Statement of Faith, field questions about that statement, and instruct all leaders to address spiritual issues from that position. If they can't agree to the New Life Statement of Faith, they can't be small-group leaders. We conclude the orientation by having each potential new leader complete an application form with references, take a personality test and a spiritual gifts test, and participate in a short interview with a zone leader.

Our district pastors review all of this information. They look over each of the references and the zone leader interview. They then conduct a Colorado State background check and make a decision about whether to approve a new leader. If a leader is not approved because of information gained through a reference or a current sin issue in his or her life, we handle it in the most life-giving way possible. We might suggest that the applicant participate in a group for a semester, serve as an assistant with a strong leader, or follow some other course of action to help be better prepared for leadership. But if an individual is approved—and most are—we assign that individual to a section leader and help him or her start planning the proposed group.

The Directory

A big part of the success of a small group initially is making sure that accurate information about each group is easily accessible. The primary tool we use is the publication of a Small-Group Directory at the beginning of each semester. Once a leader is approved, he or she submits a Small-Group Directory Form that includes all of the necessary information needed to go into the directory: the name of the group, the topic, the date and location of the meetings, contact information, and any potential costs.

All of this information is compiled, printed, and passed out at church at the beginning of each semester. It is also available online (see www.newlifechurch.org for the current example).

Rally Week

Operating on a semester format means that there are defined stopping and starting times for small groups. Our semesters are determined by the distinct calendar mechanisms that exist within the culture of our city—for example, the school calendar for the largest school district in our city. Therefore, we have three semesters of unequal length throughout the year. Our fall semester runs from September through December; our spring semester runs from January through mid-May; a shorter summer semester runs from June through August.

When we moved to this semester format, we were concerned that we might be hindering long-term relationship potential. But it's never been a problem. People develop close friendships much more quickly when they gather around a common interest, and even people who only attend a small group only for the length of one semester often become permanent friends. Furthermore, about 85 percent of our groups continue to meet from one semester to the next. The starting and stopping points give people a certain comfort going in, because they know there will be a clearly defined exit point between semesters should they want to leave the group, and a starting point to join another group. Also, leaders have a chance to take a semester breather from time to time in this system. We are just now beginning to see the ebb and flow of leaders in, out, and back in.

Because of these starting and stopping points, there is a definite need to kick off each new semester in a big way. The first week of the break between semesters is a week we call Rally Week. In that week, our whole staff works to promote small groups. Rally Week provides us the opportunity to create a lot of excitement for small groups, and we use a series of big events to do this. They are on the church schedule far in advance so we can make sure nothing competes with them. Here's how we do it:

Rally Week runs from Sunday to Sunday, with a different event attracting different segments of people each night. We may start off with an emphasis on marriage and family on Sunday, followed by a men's rally event on Monday, a women's rally event on Tuesday, something for youth on Wednesday, a singles' rally event for Thursday, and then a Prime Ministers' rally on one of the weekend days. Those events are planned within the zones to attract their particular demographic: We've had Gary Smalley come speak to the couples; a coffee-house comedy night has marked the rally event for the young professionals; and Tony Evans has charged our men's section. Whatever the event, we try to build it in a way that attracts people inside and outside of New Life Church. Flyers and radio and newspaper ads help get the word out.

At each event, tables are lined up and down the main hallway of our building. Small-group leaders who lead groups that might attract the segment of people attending the event host each table. The leaders make up their own flyers, decorate their tables, and perhaps bring food and inexpensive give-away items to attract people to stop by their tables. When people come to the table, they can learn about the small group and give the leader contact information if they're interested.

At the conclusion of Rally Week, I teach a message during the weekend services stressing the importance of relationships in the body of Christ. I encourage everyone to sign up for a small group. The week immediately after Rally Week is a preparation week allowing leaders to compile lists of people interested in their groups, make phone calls, etc. The week after that, the groups begin to meet.

What Happens in Small Groups?

In our early years of small group ministry, we thought that every group should do everything—develop relationships, disciple people, and reach out to the lost community. When we first realized that it wasn't all happening in every group, we thought we should make it happen. So, we tried to develop programs to force all those activities. The groups plodded through our discipleship and outreach programs with very little passion and very little impact. No thanks! I don't want to do that again.

Now we realize that discipleship and outreach flow out of relationships and that each small group has a unique makeup that causes it to excel in a specific area. During an orientation class one Sunday afternoon, a man came up to me and said, "The only thing I do well is repair collectible cars. How can I be a small-group leader?" After talking about it a little and developing the idea, he started a small group called "Auto Mechanics 101." The first semester he led this group, twenty-eight people joined to learn how to repair their cars. Sometime during the semester, the members of the group decided to start an emergency car-repair service for the widows and single moms in our church. They did it all—scheduled the repairs, did the work, and blessed people. If we had tried to drive this idea, it almost certainly never would have flourished. But when people developed the passion naturally, genuine helps ministry occurred.

Every small-group leader knows his or her purpose is to help each person in a group move one step up the Engel Scale every semester. That's it. Their purpose is simple and clear. We encourage them to do one of four things at each meeting—worship, prayer, Bible study, or a testimony. This requirement is very plausible in most any group setting. And it recognizes that the type and spiritual level of a person who is attracted to a hiking group may be very different from the person attracted to a Bible study or prayer group.

LEADERSHIP TRAINING

There are two common myths about training small-group leaders. Myth #1 is that leaders must be fully competent and trained *before* leading a group. Myth #2 is that training leaders is based entirely upon detailed skill-level instruction. When we first started training leaders, we required an eight-week training program on Saturdays to be completed *before* leading a group. When we saw how prohibitive that was, we whittled it down to two weeks, then to a Sunday afternoon, then to the simple orientation and ongoing training through regular meetings and relationships.

We conduct leadership training meetings on the first Sunday evening of each month during the semester. We've tried every Sunday night, but it's too burdensome to most leaders' busy schedules. The first thirty minutes are spent in a general session that includes a short time of praise and worship and a teaching on leadership from me, one of the other pastors, a zone leader, or perhaps a special speaker. Then we break up into districts for thirty minutes, and each district pastor either teaches or leads a discussion. The last hour is spent in section huddles, where each section leader spends time discussing the topic for the evening or addressing other issues. Each group also spends time in prayer for one another and for others in their groups.

What About Reports?

Naturally, we'd like to be able to measure our success in quantitative ways. However, requiring reports unintentionally encourages leaders to think in quantitative rather than relational terms. When we tried to enforce a weekly reporting form in triplicate, we found that leaders tended to minister toward that report. In the end, the reports served no viable purpose outside of making us feel as though we had some control over what was happening.

We now provide a group roster form that each leader turns in about six weeks into each semester. This roster simply lists the names, phone numbers, and E-mail addresses of the people regularly attending the group, along with a few demographic questions about the group. This adequately provides us with a measure of the number of people within our congregation who are connected in a small group, as well as a measure of the number of people in the outside community who are participating. That's enough for us. We know good ministry is happening because our small-group, section, and zone leaders are talking about it in their regular meetings with district pastors.

SHOULD EVERYONE BE IN A SMALL GROUP?

When we started free-market small groups, I was careful not to tell our departments that they had to change what they were doing. But all of our departments have found ways to incorporate small-group thinking into their designs. The praise-and-worship ministry at New Life involves approximately three hundred people. This is a ministry that requires a significant commitment on the part of each member. Instead of telling the people who are committed to this ministry that they *also* need to be in a small group, in addition to volunteering with the praise and worship team, we worked to make the praise-and-worship ministry a place where people could develop relationships. After all—they were already associated with a project that interested them and were with people of like interests. Our worship pastor, Ross Parsley, has structured the rehearsal night so it allows for a full choir rehearsal as well as time spent in small groups. Sometime during the evening of rehearsal each week you'll find small groups of choir members and musicians meeting in rooms, stairwells, and hallways throughout our church building.

Our junior-high, high-school, and college departments have very powerful ministries to the youth of our church and our community. They have a large youth meeting on Wednesday nights that serves a similar purpose to our large weekend services. In addition, a series of small groups led by teens meet in homes throughout the week with the assistance of a youth sponsor. Our youth pastors have weekly leadership meetings with the teen leaders for the purposes of teaching and training. Youth small groups delve into everything from rock climbing to drama to traditional Bible studies, and many have a strong draw among nonbelieving teens.

The children's ministry at New Life Church looks a lot like traditional Sunday school. On Sunday mornings and evenings, our children's small groups meet in age-appropriate classes just as they would in any other Sunday-school program. They are natural small groups. But what about the children's small-group leaders? Like people in the worship ministry, they have already made a significant commitment. Instead of changing what works successfully for kids, Kevin Moore, the children's pastor, has developed ways to make teaching Sunday school an opportunity to connect with a few other people who enjoy teaching children. Simple things, such as making doughnuts and coffee available in a place where leaders can connect with other teachers before class, or developing quarterly training meetings on Saturdays so teachers can spend the day with section leaders, help make this a place where children's small-group leaders develop relationships with people who share a similar passion.

The examples are endless, but the point is that we make opportunities available for people to connect in small groups where they are rather than placing an additional time requirement on them. Small-group ministry doesn't have to develop a model that all departments must serve—it's OK for it to look a little different in each department.

IN SUMMARY

In an age when our culture is undergoing constant change, small-group ministry has to remain as dynamic as every other aspect of church ministry. The fruits of free-market small-group ministry far exceed the risks involved in being willing to release ministry into the hands of the saints to do the work of the ministry. It's totally and completely worth it! If we are bold enough to take the chance and let the members of our churches fulfill the callings that the Lord has placed on their lives, the ministry that flows out of our churches will go beyond anything we could ever design.

So, what should you do? Start. You have a group of people around you who have wonderful ministries inside them. Equip them. Prepare them. Empower them. And you'll have a wonderful ministry. Let's go!

CHAPTER FIFTEEN

A Special Word for Pastors and Church Leaders

From Pastor Ted Haggard with Ted Whaley,
Director of Small-Group Ministry
at New Life Church:
Ten Things We Don't Have to Do

PASTOR, I'M WRITING YOU TODAY FROM A CRAMMED CABIN OF a Delta jet between Dallas and Colorado Springs. It's Friday night, I'll see my family tomorrow morning, and then I'll preach three times this weekend. I think I'm probably a lot like you in that my plate is full, I've got plenty to do, and I don't want to do anything just because it sounds good. I want to do things that work.

That's why this chapter is addressed specifically to you. I know you are called, that you want your church to function well, and that you know that the way we minister to the people in our churches will not only influence their lives, but will also impact our lives and our families. We carry a tremendous responsibility, a constant pressure. If we do a good job in our churches, people's lives will be better. Doors will open for us in our communities and in our futures. The kingdom of God will expand in our cities and towns. If we do a poor job, or do a job that is perceived by others to be a poor job, then people receive the brunt of it. Futures are impacted. Eternities are in the balance. Our options as pastors narrow.

Ours is one of just a few jobs that carry stakes so high. So trust me when I say that I know how apprehensive you may be to more change. I know how precious is the weight that you carry.

I don't want your options to narrow. I want your greatest dreams to be realized. I want your horizons to broaden. I want your church to grow. I want your people to be happy, successful, and vibrant. I aim for your success, and I want you to know that. That's why this final chapter is written specifically to you in the form of "things we don't have to do anymore." It's because I know that you work hard, but I'm convinced that you are probably doing some things that aren't the most productive. I think there are better uses of your time than much of what concerns you. Noble and valiant as they are, there are many things that *you don't have to be doing.*

I've shown you how wonderful and effective the move to a free-market small-group culture has been for our church. Are you convinced yet? I hope so, because I think many of the ideas in this book will make your church more effective *and* your life much easier. Now, I know there are many good ideas out there. Lots of people are offering you a system or a program or an eight-step path to bigger, better, more effective ministry. And they might work to some extent. But we have services to run, people to help, staff to lead, events to plan—not to mention spouses to love and children to raise. There's only so much of us to go around. We'd love to do the eight-step plan, but who's got the time and energy?

I like the free-market approach because, in addition to making church better, it makes life easier. It doesn't add any more work to your schedule.

Instead, it opens the door for all of us to work on the priority items that we need to be focusing on. As pastors, we need *less* to do, not more.

So, friends, there's one last thing you need to know (take a deep breath and prepare to exhale a long, slow sigh of relief): As good as free-market ministry has been for our church, *it's been best of all for my staff and me.* The reason for this is that New Life's transition to free-market small groups has led to much of the load of ministry being spread across our entire congregation. Whew . . . Now no one is being overburdened; no one is being stretched too thin; no one is burning out. No ulcers. No carrying the weight of the world on our shoulders. No sleepless nights spent tossing and turning trying to figure everything out ourselves. I'm telling you, I think it has actually kept all my hair in place and slowed down the aging process!

Are you ready for a breath of fresh air? I'm going to take this final chapter to point out for you ten things that I think are significantly different now, in the free-market era here at New Life—*ten things that we don't have to do.*

1. COME UP WITH NEW IDEAS

We no longer have to constantly come up with new ideas to meet the growing and diverse needs of our congregation. Before we moved to a small-group-based church, my staff was quickly becoming exhausted trying to manage all of the programs that we had put into place to meet the needs of our congregation. As our congregation continued to grow, the challenge of managing those programs while trying to develop new ones was almost impossible. Now, 95 percent of the ministry flowing from New Life Church starts with the idea of one person or a group of people. The free-market concept fosters creativity and innovation in every member, and the types of groups are so diverse that almost every need I could think of is met through a small group of one type or another. The role of the pastor has shifted from managing programs to equipping leaders to do the work of the ministry.

2. BE EXPERTS

Pastors no longer have to be experts in everything. Now the "experts" are leading small groups in their areas of expertise—imparting their strengths into the lives of people who are weak in those areas. Instead of having to be experts in dealing with all of life's struggles, we can easily connect someone with another individual who has the same interest or need and has demonstrated success in it.

For example, if a couple comes in struggling because of bad financial management, I don't necessarily have to put on my financial analyst cap and solve their dilemma. Instead, I can encourage them to connect with other believers in the body who can speak wisdom into their lives, and direct them to one of the various family-finance small groups.

3. SPEND HOURS COUNSELING

Pastors no longer have to spend countless hours in pastoral counseling. As New Life Church continued to grow, my pastoral staff felt an increasing frustration over the fact that they were not able to know and be a part of the lives of every member. Many of them spent the majority of their time in their offices counseling the few most troubled individuals—usually those who had no connection in the Body. At one point, depending on the urgency, an individual might have to wait two to three weeks to see a pastor.

Now, my associate pastors spend an average of one full day or two half-days a week in pastoral counseling. The types of individuals seeking a pastor, for the most part, are still those who have not connected with others. The majority of the pastoral care of New Life members is being handled at the small-group-leader or section-leader level. Many more serious cases involving divorce, suicide, etc., are handled at the zone-leader level. With the leaders connecting with and counseling the people, my associates have more time to spend in the development and pastoral care of the leaders.

4. MICROMANAGE DETAILS

Pastors no longer have to micromanage the details of their areas of ministry. The free-market concept allows for maximum individual freedom and flexibility. Believers can step out and be empowered in their areas of expertise, interest, and/or need, as well as in their areas of gifting and passion. The role of the pastor is to equip the leaders and facilitate their ministries. The pastor is no longer in the position of having to plan, coordinate, and approve or disapprove every detail of ministry, but rather to empower and direct others in ministry.

In the chapter entitled "Nuts & Bolts," I told several stories of individuals who each started a small group with a very novel idea (e.g., auto mechanics and clowning). Either of these ideas would have been squashed under a traditional view of ministry. But by releasing ministry into the lives of these people, their ministries under the covering of New Life Church have progressed far beyond anything I could have planned or tried to manage.

5. PUSH PEOPLE UPSTREAM

We no longer have to "push people upstream." Before we moved into free-market small groups, we often found ourselves trying to talk people into doing things that we wanted them to do to fulfill our vision. Now, we're helping them fulfill *their* visions, and it's much easier and more fun. A big part of my vision for New Life Church is to equip our members to do the work of the ministry.

Many pastors today are "swimming upstream" with their congregations, feeling frustrated with the lack of response from their members. At New Life, they come out of the woodwork to participate in real ministry in the body and in our community, because it's ministry based on their ideas and their passion! As pastors, we're swimming *with* them instead of *against* them!

6. DELAY MINISTRY

No longer do we have to delay ministry because of cumbersome boards and policies. Free-market small-group leaders all go through the same process to become leaders—attending an orientation, committing to the job description, receiving on-going training, and adhering to a lifestyle honor code and the creed of New Life Church. In addition, each one has demonstrated a track record as verified by three references. Once leaders are approved, it becomes my goal to ensure their success—linking them in with section leaders who can coach and encourage them in ministry. If they have met all the criteria to be approved as a small-group leader, then they work with their section leaders to make it happen.

Many churches get tangled up in time-intensive boards and policies that delay or altogether prevent ministry from getting off the ground. I can honestly say that I am fully aware of the fact that I am *not* aware of everything that is happening in the New Life Church body and our community as the result of ministry through New Life Church small groups, and I love that!

7. FEEL ALONE

No one has to feel alone in ministry. At New Life Church, I consider everyone a leader or a potential leader. My members know this, and I believe that our entire congregation senses a real partnership in ministry—all doing very different things, but accomplishing a common goal. I have instilled a very strong sense of the impact that we can make as a corporate body, stressing the importance of remaining connected, attending weekend services, and worshiping together. But throughout the week, New Life Church small-group ministry is happening at all times and days of the week—at our church building and throughout our city—in people's living rooms, factory cafeterias, and the neighborhood Starbucks.

The emphasis that we place on ministry coming from relationships is reinforced by the effort that we make to ensure tight relationships between small-group leaders and their section leaders. When we do something as a corporate body, such as our Christmas and Easter outreach productions, we don't have to beg for volunteers. All of our small groups band together and get the job done—building sets, making costumes, acting, dancing, greeting, and cleaning. There is no sense of small groups competing with anything else, because they are the priority. When I need to call on them to help us do something big together, they are ready to respond.

8. MANDATE DISCIPLESHIP OR EVANGELISM

We no longer have to mandate a special discipleship or outreach emphasis. Before free-market small groups, we tried all sorts of outreach programs to reach the lost in our community. While they were not a total failure, we were often asking people to do something totally unnatural to them, not to mention the people in our community. Even when we followed a more traditional form of small groups, we often felt that we weren't toeing the line when it came to discipleship and evangelism. Now we are doing both well.

I believe that true discipleship isn't a program of memorizing important facts about the Christian faith, but rather it is the result of a relationship—living our lives side by side with other believers. It is modeling what they do well and living our lives better, making better decisions, and becoming more Christlike in our behavior. With almost 67 percent of our congregation involved in at least one small group, I know that this is happening. The pastoral counseling load proves it! The quality of lives being lived by most of my congregation proves it! When it comes to reaching the lost, there is no other way I can account for baptizing more than 750 people this past year!

Besides our Christmas and Easter outreach efforts, the primary door into faith in Christ and into New Life Church is through a small group. In fact, the small groups that most of us would consider to be the least "spiritual" are really the most evangelistic. I have heard countless stories of people coming to Christ through volleyball, scrapbooking, hiking, four-wheeling, and rock climbing.

9. COAX PEOPLE

We no longer have to coax people into joining a small group. I have already bared my soul and admitted to you that, prior to free-market ministry at New Life, small groups weren't very appealing to me. That begs the question, *Why would they be of interest to anyone else?* We had the idea that "one size fits all," but we learned that ministry works better when there are many sizes. When we heard from our own members that the two things keeping them from being in a small group were the lack of relevance and the indefinite time commitment, we knew the move toward free-market small groups was right. It's the way people in a free-market culture think.

Now, New Lifers are going to groups that interest them, meet a specific need they are facing, or connect them with people in a similar stage of life. They are going because they want to, not because I'm telling them to.

10. RECRUIT LEADERS

We no longer have to recruit leaders. In the first two years of doing traditional small-group ministry, we quickly hit a brick wall. In 1994, as a church of almost forty-five hundred people, we could develop only eighty leaders, and connect less than a thousand of our members in those eighty groups. With highly managed and controlled small groups, we had to beg and twist arms to get people to lead. Once we gave up the need to manage and control ministry, and began empowering people to do the work of the ministry, the result was amazing. Now we have a leadership pool of more than a thousand leaders. They are ministering in the areas of their own passion and gifting, and they're doing it willingly. In fact, I've reached the point that if I, or my pastors, has to twist someone's arm to do something, I have a pretty good sense that it's not worth doing.

In addition, the semester format provides some breathing room for leaders and small-group members alike. It recognizes that we all need to take a break from time to time, or that a change in our stages of life or circumstances may move us into a different season of ministry. Other than a reminder from the pulpit about upcoming Small-Group Leader Orientations and a poster or two in the main hallway of our church, we don't actively recruit small-group leaders. It's not that we're lazy or have any philosophical objection to it; it's that we don't have to. They step up to the plate, semester after semester, and volunteer to fulfill their ministry callings. In fact, every semester, more than a hundred people attend the orientation—considering small-group leadership as the place to fulfill their vision for ministry.

Yesterday I met with a pastor who was desperately trying to serve his church, but every move he made to try to strengthen the church was counterproductive. As a result, he was actually losing members who had a history of faithful service in the church. He was a sharp man, and very pleasant. But because his church was declining and because of the disappointment and hurt from some of those who left the church, he was considering resigning.

The church's trouble was not a result of anything *he* wasn't doing. No, he'd been working hard. In fact, he'd been the center of the church's ministry—there was too much pressure on him. I asked him to stop. I asked him to equip his people to do the ministry. He'd already been preaching this idea, but didn't have a structure that would work to facilitate the members of his church.

After an hour's discussion about a few of the principles you've just read, he saw that he didn't need to be excessively cautious about everyone. He realized that instead, he could give the people in his church permission to begin serving others. At the beginning of our conversation, he was quite discouraged. By the end, he had hope and knew what to do.

I predict that within three months his church will start growing, and that within a year he'll be consumed with managing God's blessing and the resulting growth rather than putting out the fires created from decline. He has a great future in church ministry because he knows how to do what God has called him to do: disciple others.

When asked to describe what it's like pastoring a church that uses free-market small groups, I always say things like *easy* and *simple*. Once the program was implemented and operating, my personal productivity increased dramatically because I gained eight hundred assistant pastors to relate throughout the city to coach people in life. I also gained the freedom to do the things I am called to do to serve New Life and the overall body of Christ. For me, if it's not simple, I won't do it. And, yes, friends, this is easy. I did it, and you can too. It'll make your church larger, stronger, and healthier, and it'll free you to do the things that only you can do in your church and community.

I have no doubts that as you apply these principles to your church, you will begin to experience the relief I've experienced. No, you don't have to be one of the greats who are known throughout the world in the body of Christ to lead a great church. But you do have to know how to empower people. I've enjoyed spending this time with you. Now you've got the idea. Start, and have fun!

Appendix

New Small-Group Leaders Orientation

With Ted Whaley,
Director of Small-Group Ministry
at New Life Church

ONCE WE MOVED FROM TRADITIONAL SMALL-GROUP MINISTRY to free-market small-group ministry, one of the most significant results that we have seen is that we no longer have to recruit (beg and arm-twist) people to lead small groups. They are coming out of the wood-work! Prior to this free-market way of thinking, we had developed a "training program" that was so prohibitive that most leaders completely lost interest before they ever had an opportunity to lead a group. Over the years, we have retooled the entry point into leadership, and it has become an inviting, enjoyable way for people to learn more about small-group leadership—answering their questions and addressing their concerns.

The entry point into small-group leadership should not set up barriers that discourage most people from making the attempt. And the goal of the entry point should not be to make people feel obligated. At the same time, it should not be designed with the idea of "screening people out."

New Small-Group Leaders Orientation is a four-hour class designed to make the first step an easy and enjoyable one. Several posters in the main hallway of our building provide a constant reminder of this "first step," with registration cards available to drop off at the Information Center anytime throughout the year. The registration card is also available on-line (www.newlifechurch.org). You'll find it located under the icon for *Small Groups Directory*, and then under *Online Forms*. The actual orientation is conducted three times a year about midway through each semester, in preparation for the coming semester.

About two weeks prior to the orientation, we send out a package of materials to each person who has registered to attend. Included in the package are an application packet, three reference letters and forms, an interview questionnaire, a DISC Personality Profile, Quest, and a letter explaining each of these components. We include an audiotape that describes free-market small-group ministry—its philosophy and structure. We ask prospective leaders to listen to the tape and complete all of the information before coming to the orientation. They then fill out a detailed application form, much like a job application, with additional information about their spiritual lives and experience in ministry. The application includes statements indicating candidates' willingness to help fulfill the purpose, mission, and vision of New Life Church, to adhere to a lifestyle honor code, to support and teach our Statement of Faith, and to fulfill the job description of a small-group leader. Applicants also sign a document giving us permission to complete a State of Colorado Criminal Background Check, and they complete the DISC Personality Profile and the Quest motivational gifts analysis. Finally, prospective leaders are asked to mail a letter and a reference form to three relationships—anyone except family members—with a return envelope back to the Small-Group Ministries Department.

By the time they arrive at the orientation, they already have an understanding of the principles of free-market small-group ministry and have all of the paperwork completed. This allows us time to address some primary things that most people want to know before they enter into leadership.

I should note that we've learned a couple of simple things about making the orientation easier to attend. We've learned that the best time for people to come to such an orientation is while they are already on the church campus! So the orientation begins right after the last Sunday-morning service. We used to let them go home for lunch, but we quickly found that the Sunday-afternoon nap or the football game often interfered. Right after the service is over, we have lunch and child care waiting for each registered prospective leader. (Requests for information regarding applicants' child care needs, lunch preferences, and any ideas for a small group, are included on the orientation registration card.)

The pace for the orientation is relatively relaxed, but fast. Each segment of the orientation is kept to twenty-minute intervals. The room is arranged in round tables set for six people—each table is hosted by a zone leader. Once people arrive and pick up their boxed lunches, they immediately begin to get acquainted with others around their tables. The zone leaders collect the interview questionnaires, and then conduct short interviews from these completed forms with each prospective new leader at their tables. This short, face-to-face interview is conducted during the breaks throughout the afternoon. Once completed, zone leaders make their notes and recommendations on these forms.

The first topic for the afternoon is entitled "Seeing Yourself as a Leader." Our goal here is twofold. First, we have found that it is important to reestablish the definition of a leader and dispel the many myths that most people believe about leaders. They need to understand that good leaders don't have to be teachers or pastors. Once the myths are corrected and people understand that they can be leaders, we discuss some of the key qualities that all good leaders share.

After a short break, we move to the second topic titled "Pastoral Care in Small Groups." During this segment we address the role of a small group leader as a pastor—caring for people. We also address some of the concerns that many people have about the whole issue of *counseling*. Many fears are eliminated when we tell people that they do not have to be—in fact, they should not call themselves—"counselors." We delineate "Three Levels of Ministry"—a way to know whether the problems and issues that members bring to leaders can be handled by them, or if they should be moved to the section- or zone-leader level. This is when they first begin to understand the importance of our structure and the chain of command. We tell prospective leaders that their primary responsibility in ministering to the needs of their members is to be able to encourage, share scripture, and pray with their members. If a problem brought to a leader requires more than that, then the leader should contact his or her section leader. We also provide a very clear understanding of the importance of confidentiality and reporting issues in cases of abuse or potential harm to oneself or others. This always raises a few eyebrows, but new leaders are relieved to learn that these types of situations are rare.

Next we move on to the topic of "Prayer in the Life of a Leader." During this session we address everything from the importance of a vital, daily prayer life for the leader to the necessity of having a prayer covering—others who pray for you as a leader. Of course, this is part of the job description for every level of small-group leadership—to pray for those above and below you in the chain of command. We close this session out with a short time of prayer around the tables, and a concluding prayer over the entire group.

At this point, everyone has a very good comprehension of the heart and philosophy of small-group ministry at New Life Church. So we move into a session titled "What's Next?" Here we outline the process for being approved as a leader, submitting the information about a small group that will become part of the next semester, and becoming part of a section of small groups. This session includes some specifics about due dates and more.

We have a small-group resource table available throughout the afternoon. Here we place some of the newer materials and curriculum for prospective leaders to peruse to gain ideas for their groups. We always try to include some of the latest study books and video series on this table.

We conclude the afternoon with a session led by me. During this session I summarize the overriding vision and philosophy of small-group ministry at New Life Church. It is this time that I spend with prospective new leaders, about forty minutes to an hour, that lays the foundation for preventing most of the problems that many in small-group ministry fear. After I validate the role of a small-group leader as that of a pastor—including the responsibility that comes with serving in that role—as well as a legal agent of New Life Church, I give a simple presentation of New Life's theology, our Statement of Faith, admonishing new leaders to adhere to it as absolute. Then I give a firm understanding of the importance of working within a chain of command—stressing how important it is to have an active relationship with a section leader. I conclude with a discussion of principles about relationships that empower one another for ministry, as I discuss in detail in my book, *The Life-Giving Church*. I then open up the remaining time for questions and answers. People always like to converse with me, asking me questions that range from practical expectations to theological insights about our Statement of Faith. This is usually a very fun, interactive closing to the afternoon. And I think that this really brings the "close" in the hearts of most people who have come not yet sure about the idea of leadership in their own lives. Once they understand just how much permission I am giving them, they grab hold with tremendous enthusiasm.

Any remaining time in the afternoon is spent finishing up interviews and turning in paperwork. The evaluations of this afternoon always come in overwhelmingly positive—it's a "fun, fast-paced, informative afternoon." Each semester, this orientation draws an average of a hundred prospective new leaders. That generates about forty-five to fifty new small groups!

Notes

Introduction

1. Robert Kriegel, *If It Ain't Broke, Break It: And Other Unconventional Wisdom for a Changing Business World* (New York: Warner, 1992).

2. John Bevere, *Under Cover Workbook & Video Series* (Nashville: Thomas Nelson Publishers, 2001).

Chapter 1

1. Charles Spurgeon, *The Quotable Spurgeon* (Wheaton: Harold Shaw Publishers, 1990), 271.

Chapter 2

1. Philip Yancey, *The Jesus I Never Knew* (Grand Rapids: Zondervan Publishing House, 1995), 88–89.

2. James F. Engel and Wilbert H. Norton, *What's Gone Wrong with the Harvest?* (Grand Rapids: Zondervan Publishing House, 1975), 45.

Chapter 4

1. Stephen E. Ambrose, *Rise to Globalism: American Foreign Policy Since 1938* (New York: Penguin Books, 1991, orig. 1971), 78.

2. DISCinsights' Biblical Personality System, Institute for Motivational Living, New Castle, Penn., 2000. Contact: www.DISCinsights.com.

Chapter 5

1. George Barna, *Growing True Disciples* (Grand Rapids: Zondervan, 1998), 8–9.

Chapter 6

1. "How Bush Rates," *Time*, 31 December 2001–7 January 2002, 123.

2. Ibid.

3. William J. Bennett, *Our Sacred Honor* (Nashville: Broadman & Holman, 1997), 84.

4. Ibid., 45.

5. Ibid., 46.

6. Kiron K. Skinner et. al, eds., *Reagan in His Own Hand* (New York: Simon & Schuster, 2001), 227.

Chapter 8

1. Dr. Martin Luther King Jr., "I Have a Dream," speech delivered on the steps at the Lincoln Memorial in Washington, D.C., on 28 August 1963.

2. Ted Haggard and John Bolin, *Confident Parents, Exceptional Teens* (Grand Rapids: Zondervan, 1999).

Chapter 9

1. Thomas Cahill, *How the Irish Saved Civilization* (New York: Doubleday, 1995), 99–119.

2. Barna, *Growing True Disciples*, 108–110.

3. Dr. Larry Crabb, *Connecting* (Nashville: Word Publishing, 1997).

Chapter 10

1. Mother Teresa, *Total Surrender* (New York: Walker and Company, 1985), 109.

2. F. Scott Fitzgerald, *The Great Gatsby* (New York: MacMillan Publishing Company, 1925), 48.

3. Stephen E. Ambrose, *Undaunted Courage* (New York: Simon and Schuster, 1996), 56–57.

Chapter 11

1. Mark Twain, *The Adventures of Tom Sawyer* (New Jersey: Watermill Press, 1980), 97–98.

2. Win Arn, Carroll Nyquist, and Charles Arn, *Who Cares About Love* (Monrovia, Calif.: Church Growth Press, 1986), 25.

3. C. S. Lewis, *Mere Christianity* (New York: MacMillan Publishing, 1943), 116.

4. Ibid., 115.

5. Twain, *Tom Sawyer*, 218–20.

About the Author

Pastor Ted Haggard founded New Life Church in 1985. It now has more than eight thousand members and is the largest church in Colorado. His influence in the areas of church growth and evangelism has been noted by Bill Moyers, *U.S. News & World Report*, *Los Angeles Times*, *New York Times*, *Chicago Tribune*, *Washington Post*, *Denver Post*, *Charisma Magazine*, ABC, NBC, the BBC, International News Network, and PBS.

He graduated from Oral Roberts University in 1978 and worked as American vice-president for World Missions for Jesus, a West German missions organization operating primarily behind the Iron Curtain and in Third World socialist countries. Before starting New Life Church, he served as associate pastor with Bethany World Prayer Center in Baton Rouge, Louisiana, where he helped to establish the Bethany Family Counseling Center.

He serves on the boards of the National Association of Evangelicals, the Colorado Springs Association of Evangelicals, Global Harvest Ministries, Every Home for Christ, and the Center For Christian-Jewish Dialogue. Pastor Haggard is also senior editorial advisor for *Ministries Today*, a monthly magazine directed to pastors and ministry leaders.

Ted Haggard is the author of *Primary Purpose*, *The Life Giving Church*, *Loving Your City Into the Kingdom* (coauthored with Jack Hayford), and *Confident Parents*, *Exceptional Teens* (coauthored with John Bolin). He has also written several personal study booklets and has many teaching series on audiotape.

In 1998, Pastor Haggard oversaw the completion of the World Prayer Center, a strategic nerve center for worldwide evangelistic prayer, located on the campus of New Life Church.

Pastor Ted and his wife, Gayle, have five children.